THE
KITTY
LEAGUE

Eddie Duncan
Union City Dodgers
1955
#6

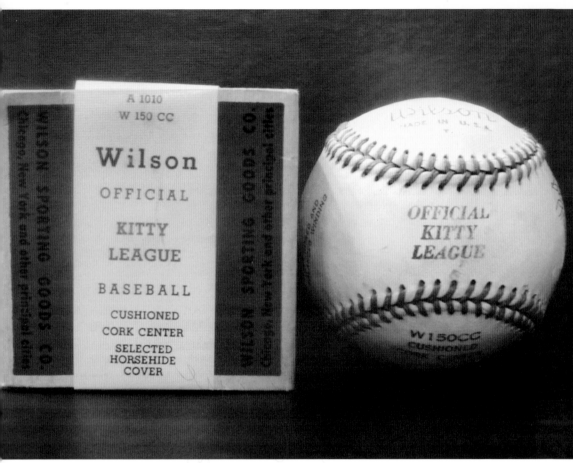

PLAY TWO! These are two rare Kitty League items: a pristine official baseball and another still in its original box. The league first adopted the Wilson ball in 1953 and used it for the last two seasons of its existence. (Kevin D. McCann collection.)

FRONT COVER: **EARL BROWNE.** Owensboro Oilers player-manager Earl Browne crouches in front of the large right-field scoreboard at Miller Field in Owensboro, Kentucky, in 1946. (Ronnie Peach.)

COVER BACKGROUND: **1947 HOPKINSVILLE HOPPERS.** The Hoppers finished in third place that year with a record of 69-56. (William Turner collection.)

BACK COVER: **1940 MAYFIELD BROWNS.** The Browns finished in sixth place in the first half and fourth place in the second half of the season with an overall record of 65-61. (Kevin D. McCann collection.)

THE
KITTY
LEAGUE

Joshua R. Maxwell and Kevin D. McCann

ARCADIA
PUBLISHING

Published by Arcadia Publishing
Charleston, South Carolina

Printed in the United States of America

Library of Congress Control Number: 2012932920

For all general information, please contact Arcadia Publishing:
Telephone 843-853-2070
Fax 843-853-0044
E-mail sales@arcadiapublishing.com
For customer service and orders:
Toll-Free 1-888-313-2665

Visit us on the Internet at www.arcadiapublishing.com

Joshua R. Maxwell:
To my wife, Sarah Maxwell, the best teammate I have ever had.
Kevin D. McCann:
In memory of my nephew Bowen Mason Lane
and my friends Dr. Curtis L. Englebright and Jim V. Bailey

CONTENTS

ACKNOWLEDGMENTS

I would like to say a very special thank you to William Turner for his dedication and enthusiastic love for history. He urged and inspired me to pursue this work, and I would not have thought of this otherwise. Also, a thank you goes to Kevin McCann for his many years of research and dedication to the preservation of the Kitty League. Also, special thanks go to all the players, family members, fans, collectors, and storytellers I have encountered. This could not have been completed without your support. To my wife, Sarah, thank you so much for your love, support, and attentive listening to the numerous stories I have told you again and again about the league. Last, but not least, a thank you goes to my son, Mason, for allowing me to be his coach and reaffirm why I think baseball is the greatest sport ever. You inspire me.

—Joshua R. Maxwell

I have had the privilege of meeting many former players and organizing two reunions for them over the past 15 years researching the Kitty League. This book would not be possible without their generosity and support. There are a few people who I would like to thank for their contributions to my research. Former player Dr. Curtis L. Englebright—who will always be "Mr. Kitty League" to me—was always willing to share a story and was gracious in offering his assistance for the reunions and contributing articles for my newsletter. Larry Edmundson has done a fine job chronicling the Union City Greyhounds/Dodgers on his website and deserves recognition. John Horne, with the Baseball Hall of Fame Library, tracked down photographs for me of major-league players. Most of all, I appreciate all the players and their families who have contributed memories and photographs for my research. Unless otherwise noted, all photographs in this book are from my personal collection.

—Kevin D. McCann

INTRODUCTION

For 31 seasons, the Kentucky-Illinois-Tennessee League—better known as the Kitty League—brought professional baseball to communities throughout western Kentucky and Tennessee, southern Illinois and Indiana, and southeast Missouri. Its name became synonymous with the minor leagues. As early as 1928, a New York sportswriter compared the "Murderer's Row" Yankees after a terrible game to "a weak-hitting Kitty League team in a bad slump." Comparing players of the 1950s to those in the 1980s, columnist Furman Bisher wrote, "There were some power hitters among them and the pitching wasn't Kitty League." St. Louis Cardinals manager and former Kitty League player Red Schoendienst, describing one umpire's interpretation of the strike zone, remarked, "Now that's not a strike in any league, not even the Kitty League."

Like the feline for which it was named, the Kitty League had many lives: 1903 to 1906, 1910 to 1914, 1916, 1922 to 1924, 1935 to 1942, and 1946 to 1955. Twenty-nine communities and cities hosted teams in Kentucky (Bowling Green, Central City, Dawson Springs, Fulton, Henderson, Hopkinsville, Madisonville, Mayfield, Owensboro, and Paducah), Illinois (Cairo, Danville, Harrisburg, Jacksonville, Mattoon-Charleston, and McLeansboro), Indiana (Evansville, Princeton, and Vincennes), and Tennessee (Clarksville, Dyersburg, Jackson, Lexington, Milan, Paris, Springfield, Trenton, and Union City).

Fans of Class D leagues such as the Kitty had to bring large doses of patience and understanding with them to the ballpark. Pitchers tended to be wild as they struggled to command their pitches, resulting in lots of walks, hit batsmen, and wild pitches. Fielders made extraordinary plays one moment and threw the ball all over the diamond the next. It was a time when being the fan of a local team was very much a personal experience. One could purchase stock in the local baseball association for as little as $10 a share and have an ownership stake. Fans opened their hearts and homes to one or more players, who paid for room and board but became more like extended members of the family.

With the passing of time and its players and fans, memories of the Kitty League are beginning to fade. It is our hope that this book will rekindle interest in each community's baseball history and the part it played in our national pastime.

Dr. Frank Bassett. It was Frank Houston Bassett who worked to bring professional baseball to western Kentucky. A native of Stephensport, Kentucky, he was an associate partner in his brother's Hopkinsville hardware business when he traveled throughout the region in January 1903 to solicit interest in a new league. On February 3, the Kentucky-Illinois-Tennessee League was organized with the towns of Henderson, Hopkinsville, Madisonville, Owensboro, and Paducah, Kentucky, as well as Cairo, Illinois. After receiving his medical degree from the University of Nashville, Bassett returned to the league he founded and served as president from 1912 to 1914, 1916, 1922 to 1924, and 1935 to 1937. His determination—and often his personal finances—would see the Kitty League through three separate "lives" during his 10-year tenure. (Bettie Bassett Clark.)

STRIKE ONE

EARLY SEASONS, 1903–1924

Spanning 186 miles from its farthest cities, the KIT League started with a dream to bring professional baseball to Kentucky, Indiana, Illinois, and Tennessee. There had been a league created seven years earlier, a short-lived independent circuit called the Pennyrile League, made up of teams in Henderson, Hopkinsville, Madisonville, and Owensboro, Kentucky, in 1896. These communities soon joined with Evansville and Washington, Indiana, to create the Kentucky-Indiana League, but it disbanded at the end of its first season.

It was not long after the KIT's inaugural season opened in 1903 that sportswriters began referring to it simply as the "Kitty" League. Just like the feline for which it was named, it would have several "lives" during its 31-year existence. Consistency was a goal the Kitty never attained during the 1903–1924 period. Four "lives" were spent, none lasting longer than five seasons: 1903 to 1906, 1910 to 1914, 1916, and 1922 to 1924. The first was defined by disorganization and infighting between league officials who threatened to tear it apart, yet it managed to survive for four seasons. Its second life from 1910 to 1914 was the most stable span and saw league founder Dr. Frank H. Bassett return as president. After attempting a comeback in 1916, it was six years before a fourth attempt to reorganize was made. It ended with a disputed second-half championship and enough hard feelings among the six clubs that the Kitty League would not return until 1935.

Despite epidemics, world war, and economic depression, fans in the region enjoyed the game and continued resurrecting the league time and again after periods of inactivity. They were eager to root for their hometown teams, such as the Hopkinsville Hoppers, Paducah Indians, Vincennes Alices, Henderson Hens, and Cairo Egyptians, and future major leaguers like Charles "Gabby" Street, Frank Shaughnessy, Hub Perdue, Larry Doyle, Edd Roush, Ervin Brame, Hank DeBerry, Guy Bush, Ben Cantwell, and Jim Turner.

1903 CAIRO EGYPTIANS. The Egyptians were the first Kitty League champions with a 67-41 record. The team played at Sportsman's Park. Its big hitters were James "Dummy" Hughes (who was deaf) and Robert Wallace, who hit at least 17 home runs. Lewis Brockett won at least 18 games and would later pitch three seasons for the New York Highlanders in 1907, 1909, and 1911.

1903 PADUCAH INDIANS. The Paddys finished the inaugural Kitty League season in fifth place with a record of 47-59. A year later, the team adopted the nickname "Indians" in recognition of the Native American chief for whom Paducah was named. Its home ballpark from 1903 to 1906 was located at Wallace Park, a popular recreational area outside town. (Sam Jackson.)

JIM HARVEY. In 1904, the Cairo Egyptians catcher caught a no-hitter pitched by Dutch Waggoner in a 5-2 win for Cairo despite the Egyptians committing six errors. One sportswriter described Harvey's banter behind the plate during a game against the Henderson Bluebirds as follows: "Harvey behind the bat, could be plainly heard above the rest, shouting, as he gave the signals, 'Come on old pal, only one left, work hard old man, that's the way, all the time coming.' " (James Pederson.)

1903 PADUCAH INDIANS STOCK CERTIFICATE. This is one of the earliest examples of a stock certificate for a Kitty League club. The Paducah Base Ball Association issued this certificate on May 29, 1903, for 49 shares at $5 each. (Sam Jackson.)

HOPKINSVILLE BASE BALL AMUSEMENT COMPANY SEAL. Displayed here is the official 1903 seal of the Hopkinsville Base Ball Amusement Company in 1903. Still in working order, the stamp is featured as part of the Hoptown Hoppers Kitty League display at the Pennyroyal Area Museum in Hopkinsville, Kentucky. (William Turner collection.)

CHARLES "GABBY" STREET. The Huntsville, Alabama, native was a catcher for the Hopkinsville Hoppers in 1903. Incomplete statistics show he batted .344 with four homers in 48 games. Street was an active player for seven seasons in the major leagues from 1904 to 1912. In 1908, he accepted a $500 bet to catch a ball dropped from the Washington Monument, though it took 13 attempts to catch it. (Joshua R. Maxwell.)

CLYDE ENGLE. Engle played third base for the Clarksville Villagers in 1903. He is best known in the majors for a pinch-hit double in the sixth game of the 1912 World Series and hitting a fly ball off Christy Mathewson that Fred Snodgrass dropped in the 10th inning. Engle scored, and the Red Sox won the World Series. (Library of Congress Prints and Photographs.)

BASEBALL!

Hopkinsville

K. I. T. League Team

vs.

Fulton

MERCER PARK

Double-Header

First Game Called 2 P. M.

Wednesday, Decoration Day, May 30th

HOPKINSVILLE GAME ADVERTISEMENT. This is an advertisement for a doubleheader at Athletic Park, Hopkinsville's first KIT League ballpark. Mercer Park was the second of three baseball parks where the Hopkinsville teams would play. It would host teams from 1910 to 1923 and 1935 to 1942. (William Turner collection.)

1904 SCORE SHEET. This is a rare unused 1904 score sheet for the Kentucky Illinois Tennessee Base Ball League. During its first season, official scorers were not paid or provided with score sheets, resulting in incomplete statistics and game information. League president William Irving Thompson made sure these mistakes were corrected in 1904, though no official statistics were published in the baseball guides until 1906.

OFFICIAL SCORE
KENTUCKY, ILLINOIS, TENNESSEE BASE BALL LEAGUE.

.... VS. .... AT .... 1904.

PLAYERS	Pos.	A.B.	R	BH	2B	SB	SH	PO	A	E	PLAYERS	Pos.	AB	R	BH	2B	SB	SH	PO	A	E
TOTALS.																					

INNINGS.	1	2	3	4	5	6	7	8	9	10	11	12	13	14	15	R	H	E

1904 PADUCAH INDIANS. The fate of the Kitty League pennant was uncertain during an off-season power struggle between league president William Irving Thompson and secretary Maurice J. Farnbaker. A Cairo supporter, Farnbaker wanted certain games in which ineligible players were used to be thrown out, thus giving the pennant to the Egyptians. Club representatives almost came to blows at a heated meeting in Cairo, after which Farnbaker—who had allegedly been removed from office—left with the league records and refused to give them up. Eventually, Paducah was awarded the championship, and Farnbaker was replaced as secretary in 1905, only to return as "acting" secretary until 1906. Pictured are, from left to right, (first row) Eddie Powers, Frank Potts, manager Johnny Ray, captain Fred Bateman, and Gus Bonno; (second row) Kitty Gerard, Dick Brahic, Jim "Buck" Freeman, ? Doll, Grover Land, ? Harley, and "Bud" Lally.

M.J. FARNBAKER
SECRETARY K.-I.-T. LEAGUE

MAURICE J. FARNBAKER. A baseball enthusiast and sports editor for the Cairo *Bulletin* newspaper, Farnbaker served as league secretary from 1903 to 1906. He was at the center of a controversial finish to the 1904 season in which both Cairo and Paducah claimed the pennant based on whether or not certain games should have been thrown out. Farnbaker continued to work on behalf of the league between 1910 and 1914.

HUB PERDUE. "The Gallatin Squash" had an 11-5 record for the Hopkinsville Browns in 1905. After the team was dropped by the league, he signed with the Vincennes Alices to finish the season. The Alices won the pennant in 1906, and Perdue had a 25-8 record with 260 strikeouts. He pitched for the Boston Braves and St. Louis Cardinals from 1911 to 1915. (Library of Congress Prints and Photographs.)

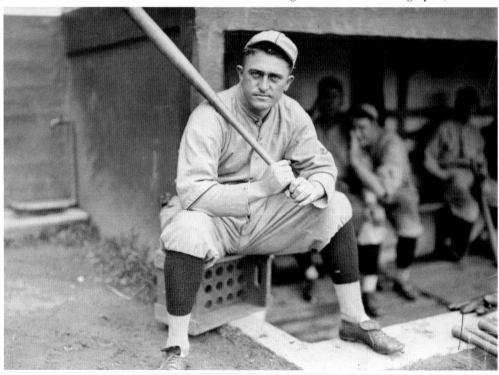

FRANK SHAUGHNESSY. "Shag" played baseball and football and ran track for Notre Dame from 1901 to 1904. To preserve his amateur status, he used the assumed name of Shannon with the Cairo Egyptians in 1904. Shaughnessy played briefly in the major leagues and later developed the Shaughnessy playoff system. He was inducted into the Kitty League Hall of Fame in 1953. (University of Notre Dame Archives.)

LARRY DOYLE. Nicknamed "Laughing Larry," Doyle played for the Mattoon-Charleston Canaries in 1906 and batted .225 with 11 triples in 91 games. A year later, his contract was purchased by the New York Giants for a then-record $4,500. He played 14 seasons, mostly with the Giants, from 1907 to 1920. (Library of Congress Prints and Photographs.)

To the Cat Box

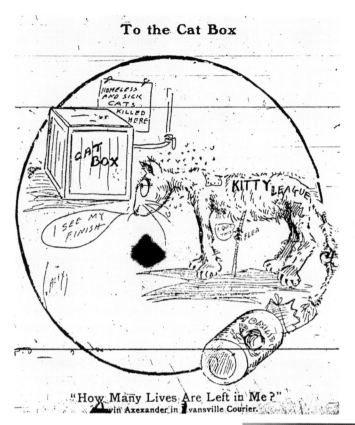

"How Many Lives Are Left in Me?"
—Wm Axexander in Evansville Courier.

KIT LEAGUE CARTOON. In 1905, the Kitty League received permission from the National Association to end its season on August 17. While the yellow fever epidemic affecting cities along the Mississippi River was cited as the official cause, some clubs used it as an excuse to stop losing money and reserve their players for the following season.

GROVER LAND. A catcher for the Paducah Indians from 1904 to 1905, Land played eight seasons for Cleveland and Brooklyn Tip-Tops. He later became a major-league coach for the Cincinnati Reds from 1925 to 1928 and the Chicago Cubs in 1929 to 1930. (Library of Congress Prints and Photographs.)

K. I. T. BASE BALL LEAGUE

ADMIT ONE

FIRST GAME JUNE 2.

Good for Any Game During the Season.

HOPKINSVILLE B. B. & A. CO

INCORPORATED

1910 HOPKINSVILLE GAME TICKET. Tickets cost 25¢ for general admission seats and 10¢ for bleachers; ladies were not charged extra. The Hopkinsville Moguls lost the June 2 season opener to the Clarksville Volunteers 10-9. (William Turner collection.)

HOPKINSVILLE MOGULS. The 1910 Hopkinsville club was called the Moguls because the Mogul Wagon Company was a major stockholder in the team. The jerseys changed from Yale grey with a maroon "H" to solid maroon with white trim and white letters spelling "Mogul" across the front. (William Turner collection.)

1910 KIT Championship. The 1910 season began with four teams: Clarksville, Paducah, Hopkinsville, and Vincennes. On July 24, McLeansboro and Harrisburg, Illinois, were added for the second half of the season. The championship playoff between first-half winner Vincennes and second-half winner McLeansboro was canceled, and both teams shared the pennant. John Nairn batted .285 for Vincennes to lead the league, and teammate Lyman Johnson won 20 victories and struck out 182 hitters.

1910 McLeansboro Miners. The Miners won the second-half pennant, but a championship series with first-half Vincennes was never played. Evansville native Clarence "Big Boy" Kraft (back row, third from left) batted .292 and hit four homers to tie for the league lead. He also led the league with a .867 winning percentage on the mound (13-2). Kraft played three games for the Boston Braves in 1914.

1911 Hopkinsville Advertisement. These are advertisements for the 1911 Hopkinsville Moguls season opener against the Clarksville Billies. The Moguls beat their cross-state rivals 5-0 in front of 1,600 fans, but the following day Clarksville returned and defeated the Moguls 11-5. Hopkinsville would win the first-half title and the 1911 Kitty League championship with a .629 winning percentage, 11.5 games over the Fulton Colonels. (William Turner collection.)

K. I. T. Baseball

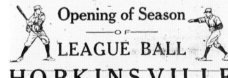

Opening of Season

—OF—

LEAGUE BALL

HOPKINSVILLE

—VS.—

CLARKSVILLE,

Wednesday and Thursday,
May 17 and 18.

GAME CALLED AT 3:30.

═══AT═══

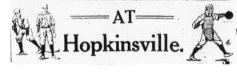

Hopkinsville.

1911 VINCENNES ALICES. Two Kentucky teams, the Fulton Colonels and Henderson Hens, and two Illinois clubs, Cairo and Harrisburg, were added in 1911. The latter transferred to Jackson, Tennessee, in the second half of the season. Although Vincennes had 4 of the top 10 batters in the league, it could not win the pennant. The Alices finished second behind Hopkinsville in the first half and sixth in the second half.

1912 CLARKSVILLE VOLUNTEERS. The league was reduced to six teams in 1912. The Clarksville Volunteers played strong all season and lost the lead only once. They were back in the lead by mid-June and finished the season in first place with a 69-29 record and .701 winning percentage.

EDD ROUSH. The 18-year-old batted .219 in 10 games for the Henderson Hens in August 1911. A year later, he played for the third-place Evansville Yankees and hit .284 in 41 games. Roush went on to become a two-time batting champion and play 18 seasons in the majors, mostly with the Cincinnati Reds. He was inducted into the Baseball Hall of Fame in 1962. (National Baseball Hall of Fame Library.)

1913 VINCENNES PLAYERS. This photograph was taken during spring training on April 22, 1913. These three players from Terre Haute, Indiana, were trying out for the Alices. From left to right are first baseman Charles Van Horn, right fielder Edgar "Ed" Withrow, and shortstop Fred Boofter. Withrow and Boofter failed to make the team, but Van Horne played in 100 games and batted .302 with 22 stolen bases.

1913 PADUCAH INDIANS. In a close race, Paducah prevailed by one game over the Clarksville Boosters to win the pennant. Art Brouthers, who had played for the Philadelphia Athletics in 1906, managed the Indians. Among Paducah's top hitters were Grady Burgess (.339, 101 runs scored, 67 stolen bases) and J.F. Whitaker (.305, 30 stolen bases). Pitchers Frank Mullin and Emmett Kuykendall both won 11 games. (Grady Burgess family.)

MAHLON HIGBEE. The 20-year-old played for the Hopkinsville Hoppers in 1922, batting .385 with 16 home runs, 101 runs scored, and 31 stolen bases. His contract was sold to the New York Giants, and he jumped from Class D ball to the major leagues in the same season. In three games, Higbee batted .400 with four hits—including a home run—and five RBIs. (National Baseball Hall of Fame Library.)

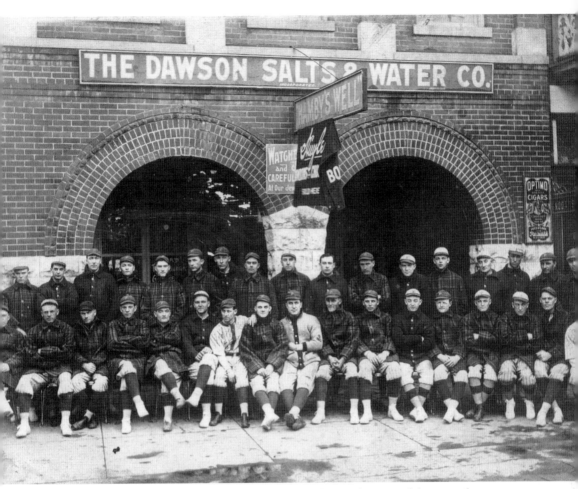

1916 PITTSBURGH PIRATES. It was not uncommon during this period for major-league teams to have spring training in Kitty League ballparks. This is a photograph of the Pirates in front of Hamby's Well at Dawson Springs, Kentucky, a community known for its healing mineral water. Fourth from the right in the second row is future Hall of Fame shortstop Honus Wagner. (Mack Sisk Collection, Dawson Springs Museum.)

EVERYBODY AND HIS BROTHER

Will be out to see the opening games of the Kitty League here

Tuesday, Wednesday, Thursday, May 15, 16 and 17.

If you don' believe it, come and see for yourself. Mayor declares a half-holiday! Parade and big brass band at 1 P. M.

Springfield vs. Hopkinsville

GAME BEGINS AT 2:30 P. M.
Admission 55 Cents.

1923 SPRINGFIELD BLANKET MAKERS. This is an advertisement for the season opener of the Springfield Blanket Makers against the Hopkinsville Hoppers. It was the only professional team that ever represented the Tennessee community. After a 14-36 record, the Blanket Makers disbanded on July 9, and the franchise was shared by Milan and Trenton, Tennessee, for the remainder of the season.

GEORGE BLOCK. A Paducah native, George Block batted .261 with 22 stolen bases as a catcher for his hometown team in 1910. He returned to the Kitty League in 1924 as player-manager of the first-half champion Dyersburg Forked Deers. After a trade to the Jackson Blue Jays, Block guided his new club into first place but dropped into second at the end. He later managed the Paducah Indians in 1937.

MEL SIMONS. "Butch" played two seasons for the Fulton Railroaders, batting .336 in 1923 and .306 in 1924. He went on to play for the Chicago White Sox in 1931 and 1932. At 41, Simons returned as player-manager of the Paducah Indians and Bowling Green Barons and hit .386 with 31 doubles and 20 stolen bases in 1940. He later managed the Fulton Lookouts for two weeks in 1955.

BEN CANTWELL. The Milan, Tennessee, native had a 7-9 record for the Paris Parisians in 1923. Three years later, he made his major-league debut with the New York Giants. Cantwell pitched for 11 seasons, 9 for the Boston Braves, and won 20 games for the Braves in 1933.

1923 OPENING DAY. On May 18, the Fulton Railroaders hosted the Dyersburg Forked Deers for their home opener at Fairfield Park. With 700 fans in attendance, Dyersburg spoiled the festivities with a 4-3 victory over the Railroaders. Fulton's Mel Simons (13th from left) went two for four

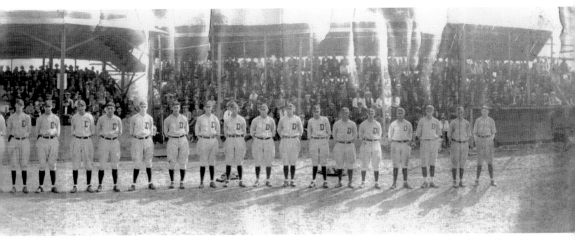

with a triple. Another future big leaguer was Jim Weaver (sixth from left). Manager Dan Griner is 18th from the left. (Mary Louise Gossum.)

PARIS PARISIANS JERSEY. Shown here is a Paris Parisians jersey worn by pitcher Jim "Milkman" Turner in 1923 or 1924. It is a grey wool flannel jersey with purple pinstripes and a large purple "P" over the left chest. The Nashville, Tennessee, native went on to pitch nine seasons for the Boston Bees, Cincinnati Reds, and New York Yankees from 1937 to 1945. (Skip Nipper.)

1924 PARIS PARISIANS. The Paris, Tennessee, club ended the first half in fourth place but took advantage of three forfeits applied to the Jackson Blue Jays to win the second-half title. It lost the championship playoff to the Dyersburg Forked Deers in four straight games. Paul Kirby led the league with a .341 batting average and 47 stolen bases. Future major leaguer Jim Turner won 16 games. (Skip Nipper.)

STRIKE TWO

DEPRESSION AND WAR, 1935–1942

Eleven years after its third life ended, the Kitty League sprang forth once again in 1935. John J. McCloskey, founder of the Texas League and a Louisville, Kentucky, native, canvassed the territory with league founder Dr. Frank H. Bassett to garner support for a revival. A six-team league was created in Kentucky (Hopkinsville and Paducah), Tennessee (Jackson, Lexington, and Union City), and Missouri (Portageville). Bassett was once again elected president.

The first two seasons ended with first-division teams exceeding the higher-classification player limit, resulting in disputed championships and no postseason playoffs. Official and complete statistics were not made available for publication in the major baseball guides of the period. It was not until the 1937 season, when the split-season format was abandoned in favor of a full-season championship and the postseason Shaughnessy playoff system was introduced (conceived by International League president and former Kitty Leaguer Frank Shaughnessy), that the Kitty League had its first undisputed champions. Franchise changes during this time included the addition of Fulton and Mayfield, Kentucky, and the relocation of the Portageville Pirates (population 1,500) to Owensboro, Kentucky (population over 25,000).

A significant leadership change was made when Dr. Bassett was ousted during a controversial league meeting at Paducah on November 17, 1937, ending the tenure of the league's founder and benefactor through 10 years and three revivals in 1916, 1922, and 1935. He was replaced by Fulton club president James Edgar "Ed" Hannephin, who resigned after the 1938 season. Ben F. Howard of Union City served from 1939 to 1940 and ended his tenure with an unusual surplus—rather than a deficit—in league funds. During his term, the Lexington, Tennessee, franchise relocated to Bowling Green, Kentucky, in 1939. Vice Pres. Shelby Peace succeeded Howard and served from 1941 until the league folded on June 16, 1942, due largely to poor attendance.

During the 1935–1942 period, the Kitty League was the proving ground for at least 36 future major leaguers. Among them were Joe Grace, Vern Stephens, Ellis Kinder, Dave Koslo, Johnny Schmitz, Ray Coleman, Johnny Beazley, George "Catfish" Metkovich, and Red Schoendienst.

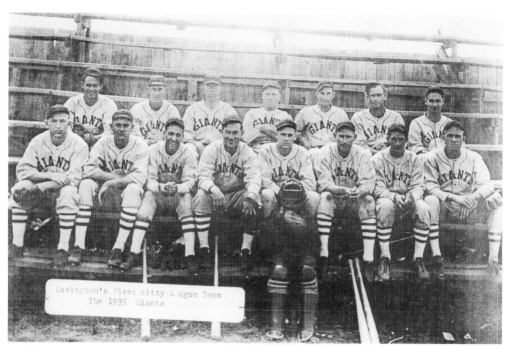

Lexington's First Kitty League Team
The 1935 Giants

1935 LEXINGTON GIANTS. Managed by 20-year-old John Antonelli, the Giants won the first-half title. They were scheduled to face the second-half winners in a championship series, but the team disagreed with the Portageville Pirates being awarded the title when the Jackson Generals and Union City Greyhounds were disqualified for exceeding the higher-classification player limit. Lexington instead played Jackson in an unsanctioned series that it lost in four straight games. (MacArthur Lewis.)

JOE GRACE. A cousin of former major-league catcher Earl Grace, the Gorman, Illinois, native batted .343 in 72 games as an outfielder for the second-division Paducah Red Birds in 1935. He went on to play six seasons with the St. Louis Browns and Washington Senators from 1938 to 1947. (National Baseball Hall of Fame Library.)

First Kitty League All-Star Team. Pictured are, from left to right, (first row) Carl Sikes, (Jackson), Budd Adams (Hopkinsville), Irwin "Spud" Wolfe (Hopkinsville), Johnny Long (Fulton), K.P. Dalton Jr. (Fulton batboy), Bobby Richards (Union City), and Norman "Kid" Elberfield (Fulton manager); (second row) John Swank (Union City), Ray Clonts (Fulton), Jesse Webb (Jackson), Lou Perryman (Mayfield), William "Buster" Morgan (Hopkinsville), Hugh Wise (Owensboro), Averette Thompson (Union City), John Wilson (Fulton), and Earl Hahn (Fulton). The Kitty League All-Stars played the Paducah Indians in front of 2,000 fans at Hook Park on July 29, 1936, and won 8-3. (Michael Perryman.)

1936 Paducah Indians. The Indians won the first-half title under former major-league pitcher Austin Ben Tincup (back row, fourth from left), who was a full-blooded Cherokee. They faced the second-half champion Union City Greyhounds in a playoff series for the pennant, but after losing the first game and seven Paducah players refusing to play because of unfulfilled financial promises made by club owner Burley B. Hook, the Indians forfeited the remainder of the series to Union City.

JUNIOR THOMPSON. A 20-game winner for Paducah, Gene Thompson and six teammates refused to play in the postseason series against Union City in 1936. They claimed the club owner never paid money promised them for winning the pennant. The players were suspended indefinitely, but the suspensions were lifted before the 1937 season. Thompson pitched in the major leagues from 1939 to 1947 and won 16 games for the world champion Reds in 1940.

GORDON SWOPE. The Paducah first baseman batted .299 with 16 home run and 86 RBIs in 1936. He is standing in front of the Indians team bus. The swastika-looking symbol worn on the front of the Paducah jersey is actually a Native American symbol that is intended to bring good luck. (Gordon Swope family.)

CLINT ANDERECK. A two-time all-star second baseman, Andereck played for the Union City Greyhounds, Lexington Giants, Bowling Green Barons, and Paducah Indians from 1935 to 1940. In 556 games, he batted .324 with 730 hits and never hit less than .300 in six seasons. He was inducted into the Kitty League Hall of Fame in 2005. (Clint Andereck family.)

1936 OWENSBORO PIRATES. On July 17, 1936, the Pirates left Portageville, Missouri (population 1,500), and relocated to Owensboro, Kentucky (population 25,000), for the second half of the season. They played at Southside Park. Pictured are, from left to right, (first row) Grundy Turlington, Alton Parker, Julian Henry, Hugh Wise, John Fitzgerald, Charles Gassaway, and Bob Helvey; (second row) business manager Billy Goff, Herbert Wilson, George Gregory, Charles Fox, Chet Clemons, Stanley Hayden, and Harry Durheim. (Ronnie Peach.)

HOPKINSVILLE HOPPERS JERSEY. The home jersey of the Hoppers used in 1936 was white wool flannel with red trim and "Hopkinsville" spelled out in red letters across the front. The uniform also included a white cap with red stripes and a bold capital "H" on the front, red stockings with white stripes, and white pants. (Pennyroyal Area Museum.)

BYLAWS AND CONSTITUTION. This little green booklet contained the rules that governed the Kitty League of professional baseball clubs in 1937. The league officers were Pres. Dr. Frank H. Bassett of Hopkinsville, Kentucky; Vice Pres. Ben F. Howard of Union City, Tennessee; and secretary Shelby Peace of Hopkinsville. Advertising throughout the booklet was paid for by A.G. Spalding & Brothers in Memphis, Tennessee, suppliers of the official league baseball.

1937 UNION CITY GREYHOUNDS. The St. Louis Cardinals farm club captured the pennant with a 73-46 record under 22-year-old all-star shortstop-manager John Antonelli. Outfielder David Bartosch won the batting title with a .337 average, and all-star pitcher George Sauer won 19 games. The Greyhounds failed to advance in the postseason Shaughnessy playoffs, dropping three straight games to the Mayfield Clothiers. Pictured are, from left to right, (first row) greyhound team mascot Fusion and batboy Billie Wagste; (second row) John Pavlige, James W. Lalumondiere, Joseph Barbieri, George Valine, Stanley Katkaveck, James Ronseieke, and Cy Redifer; (third row) David Bartosch, Edward Murphy, George Sauer, Ray Zimmerman, Paul Price, and John Antonelli. (George Valine.)

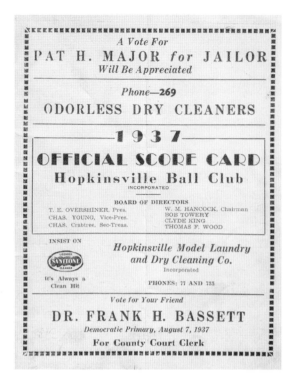

1937 HOPKINSVILLE HOPPERS SCORECARD. Shown here is the official scorecard for the Hopkinsville Ball Club Incorporated with the board of directors listed. It features an advertisement to vote for Kitty League president Dr. Frank H. Bassett for re-election as Christian County clerk. The back has an advertisement for Goff's Arena on East Ninth Street, where future Hoppers owner Billy Goff promoted wrestling matches each week in the 1930s and 1940s.

DEACON AND THE RABBIT. With a runner on first base during a game in Hopkinsville on August 2, 1937, Hoppers pitcher Victor "Deacon" Delmore noticed a rabbit near the shortstop position. He threw the ball, but it missed the rabbit. The ball went into left field, and the runner took off for second but was sent back to first base. Umpires Ellis Beggs and Don Karcher ruled that time had been called—though no one remembered it being done—and the game resumed with no quarrel from the Paducah Indians dugout. Delmore later became a National League umpire from 1956 to 1959. (National Baseball Hall of Fame Library.)

MONUMENTAL CATCH. A ballpark bet prompted Hopkinsville Hoppers all-star outfielder Art "Whitey" Grangard to stand underneath the Jefferson Davis Monument in nearby Fairview, Kentucky, on July 27, 1937, and attempt to catch a baseball dropped from the top window of the 351-foot-tall structure. After missing the first four balls and almost catching the next three, he finally snagged the eighth and ninth balls, though he had hurt his hand on one of the failed catches. The photograph below shows Grangard presumably shaking hands with the man who dropped the balls from the top. Former Hopkinsville catcher Charles "Gabby" Street performed the same stunt at the 555-foot-tall Washington Monument in 1908. (William Turner collection.)

BALLPARK ENGINEER. A Campbellsville, Kentucky, native, Hugh Wise was instrumental in bringing professional baseball back to Owensboro, Kentucky. A Purdue University graduate with a degree in engineering, Wise designed and oversaw the construction of Miller Field, which was considered one of the finest Class D ballparks of its time. He later served as a major-league scout and designed spring-training sites for the Milwaukee Braves in Myrtle Beach, Florida, and Waycross, Georgia, and the Chicago White Sox in Sarasota, Florida. (Ronnie Peach.)

HUGH WISE. Wise was a switch-hitting catcher originally signed by the Brooklyn Robins who played in two major-league games for the Detroit Tigers in 1930. In six seasons as player-manager for Owensboro, he batted .283 with 268 RBIs in 566 games. His 376 managerial victories are the most in Kitty League history. (Ronnie Peach.)

MILLER FIELD. A month before opening day in 1937, local oil producer Julius C. Miller helped raise $16,000 to build a ballpark for the Owensboro Oilers at Eighteenth and Triplett Streets. Work progressed for 26 days and nights before the first game was played on May 20. Originally called Owensboro Recreational Corporation (OCR) Field, it was renamed Miller Field to honor the club president at the end of the season. (OAMSH.)

SCOREBOARD CONSTRUCTION. This photograph shows the large, iconic scoreboard under construction in right field. It contained three apartments that were rented to tenants. Along with the modern concrete and steel grandstand, Miller Field became *the* showcase ballpark for the Kitty League. In 1940, Joe DiMaggio called it "the best minor-league park in the United States." (Owensboro Area Museum of Science and History.)

1937 MAYFIELD CLOTHIERS. The Clothiers finished in fourth place after a tie-breaking playoff game against the Jackson Generals and won the Shaughnessy playoff title. Pictured are, from left to right, (first row) Louis Perryman, Russell Goff, Len Schulte, Carl Barnhart, Joe Bordoni, Bud Caughtry, and Blaine Henkel; (second row) Vincent "Moon" Mullen, Eddie O'Connell, Elmer Wright, club president D.E. Hutchinson, Walter Holke, club secretary Milton Eckles, Jerome Witte, Paul Gunter, Clarence Springer, and Carroll Campbell.

1938 HOPKINSVILLE HOPPERS. The Hoppers captured their first championship in 1938. All-star Hal Peck (back row, second from left), who had a .331 average, led the league with 125 runs scored and 16 triples. Manager Richard P. "Red" Smith (front row, second from right), who played one game for the New York Giants in 1927, was an assistant football coach for the Green Bay Packers and New York Giants. He was later a coach for the Chicago Cubs. (Arleen Ireland.)

1938 MAYFIELD BROWNS. The St. Louis Browns farm club managed by former major-league catcher Benny Tate (second row, fourth from right) finished in fourth place. Floyd Baker (first row, fourth from left), who led the team with his .346 average and 85 RBIs, would play 13 seasons in the major leagues. Gilbert Bruhn won 18 games, and rookie Frank Biscan later played for the St. Louis Browns.

1938 MAYFIELD BROWNS SCHEDULE. Pocket schedules were a convenient way for the local club to promote its home games. This is one of the earliest examples for a Kitty League team.

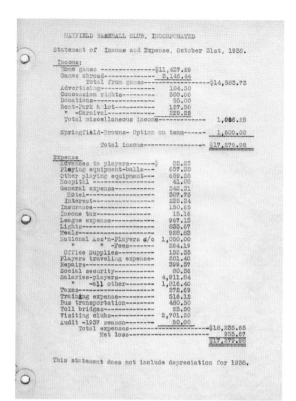

```
MAYFIELD BASEBALL CLUB, INCORPORATED

Statement of Income and Expense, October 31st, 1938.

Income:
  Home games --------------$11,427.29
  Games abroad------------   3,146.44
     Total from games----------------$14,583.73
  Advertising--------------     184.50
  Concession rights--------     500.00
  Donations----------------      55.00
  Rent-Park & lot----------     127.50
    "   -Carnival---------      229.25
  Total miscellaneous income-----------  1,096.25
  Springfield-Browns- Option on team------  1,600.00
        Total income----------------- $17,279.98

Expense
  Advances to players-------$      32.25
  Playing equipment-balls---     657.38
  Other playing equipment---     659.28
  Hospital -----------------      41.00
  General expense-----------     342.31
    Hotel------------------      307.73
    Interest----------------     235.34
  Insurance-----------------     150.65
  Income tax----------------      15.16
  League expense------------     967.13
  Lights--------------------     833.67
  Meals---------------------     928.83
  National Ass'n-Players d/c  1,050.00
    "      "     -Fees------     264.19
  Office Supplies-----------     133.35
  Players traveling expense-     261.40
  Repairs-------------------     399.37
  Social security-----------      80.36
  Salaries-players----------   4,911.64
    "     -all other--------   1,816.40
  Taxes---------------------     272.69
  Training expense----------     516.12
  Bus transportation--------     480.50
  Toll bridges--------------      23.50
  Visiting clubs------------   2,701.20
  Audit -1937 season--------      50.00
       Total expenses--------------$18,235.65
              Net loss-------------------    955.67
                               $17,279.98

This statement does not include depreciation for 1938.
```

MAYFIELD BROWNS FINANCIAL STATEMENT. This rare profit and loss statement shows the expenses involved in operating a typical Class D minor-league team in the 1930s. The Mayfield club lost $955.67 in 1938; adjusting for inflation, it would be almost $15,000 in modern funds.

1938 PADUCAH INDIANS. The fifth-place St. Louis Cardinals farm club featured future Redbirds Ray Sanders and Augie Bergamo, who won the batting title (.355). Pictured are, from left to right, (first row) Augie Bergamo, Escal Burnett, Joe Masters, Art "Whitey" Grangard, Eddie Patron, Doug Pharo, and Orville Dantic; (second row) Pete Mondino, Malcolm Matthews, Joe Barbieri, David Howe, Chauncey Scott, Vernon Horn, Ray Sanders, Jim Steger, and Spencer Woodill; Leo Fields is the batboy. (Lendell Fullerton.)

PADUCAH INDIANS LETTERHEARD. This letterhead was used by Indians general manager R.L. Myre for team correspondence in 1938.

1938 JACKSON GENERALS. The Generals finished in second place and met Hopkinsville in the playoffs. Glen Dacus won a league-best 22 games. The men pictured are, from left to right, (first row) Herbert "Dutch" Welch, Elmer Wenning, Porter Witt, Sam Glenn, Glen Dacus, Lester Gray, and Jesse Webb; (second row) Dick Jones, Lou Perryman, William "Buster" Morgan, Vincent "Moon" Mullen, Mel Merkel, Fred Walker, Archie Williams, and C.C. "Cy" Miller. (Albert Merkel.)

1938 OWENSBORO OILERS. The Oilers finished in sixth place. All-star Glenn Grimes hit .321 with 33 stolen bases. Pictured are, from left to right, (first row) Johnny Newman, Eddie O'Connell, Kendall "Kickie" Wise (batboy), Hugh Wise, and Herb Allen; (second row) Glen Levan, Jim Kell, Herb Wilson, Mel Riebe, and Bud Sly; (third row) George Brumfield, Gino Marionetti, Johnny Durda, Mel Allen, Fred Harig, Russo Sumner, and Glen Grimes. (Ronnie Peach.)

FAIRFIELD PARK. This rare c. 1938 photograph shows advertising signs on the outfield fence and the scoreboard in right-center field at Fairfield Park in Fulton, Kentucky. (Dianne Cundiff.)

FAIRFIELD PARK DUGOUT. Here is a glimpse into the home-team dugout at Fairfield Park. Fulton Eagles player-manager Ray Clonts is looking at the camera. The team finished in seventh place in 1938, and Willard Padgett was named to the Kitty League All-Star Team. (Dianne Cundiff.)

THE KITTY LEAGUE

1939 MAYFIELD BROWNS. The Browns finished a game and a half ahead of the Bowling Green Barons and Owensboro Oilers to capture the pennant with a record of 76-49. Vern Stephens, Charlie Metro, and Jim Russell were future major leaguers. Russell spent 10 seasons with the Pittsburgh Pirates and Boston Braves from 1942 to 1951. The men pictured are, from left to right, (first row) Benny Tate, Enair Hoisve, Claude Williams, Ben Kneupper, Charles Holtmeyer, Bud Williams, Bill Scott, and Vernon Stephens; (second row) club secretary-treasurer Joseph Tripp, Fred "Fritz" Klann, Arnold "Dutch" Funderburk, Jim Russell, Joe Morjoseph, Bill Harrington, Russell Goff, Charlie Metro, Edward Lanfersieck, and business manager Delton Dodds.

VERN STEPHENS. In addition to hitting 30 home runs, the 19-year-old power-hitting shortstop also won the batting and RBI titles (.361, 123 RBIs) for Mayfield in his first full professional season in 1940. Stephens played 15 years and hit 247 home runs in the major leagues, most notably with the St. Louis Browns and Boston Red Sox. He was inducted into the Kitty League Hall of Fame in 1953.

CHARLIE METRO. The Mayfield outfielder batted .256 with 14 home runs and 75 RBIs. He later played for the Detroit Tigers and Philadelphia Athletics from 1943 to 1945. Metro was part of the "college of coaches" who took turns managing the Chicago Cubs in 1962 and led the Kansas City Royals in 1970. (Photograph by Trace Kirkwood.)

MILLER FIELD OPENING-DAY FESTIVITIES. The Owensboro Oilers and the visiting Hopkinsville Hoppers celebrate opening day on May 4, 1939. The image above shows Oilers manager Hugh Wise accepting a good-luck floral horseshoe and Hoppers manager Harry Griswold a floral "H" on behalf of their respective teams. The photograph below shows both teams with caps off their heads as the flag is being raised in center field and "The Star Spangled Banner" is played by the local high school band. The Oilers (75-51) finished in a second-place tie with the Bowling Green Barons but lost three straight games to the Barons in the initial Shaughnessy playoff round. Four players—first baseman Eddie O'Connell (.314), shortstop Don DeVault (.312, 75 RBIs), outfielder Jack DeVincenzi (.344), and pitcher Howard Schumacher (22-5, 2.49 ERA)—were named to the Kitty League All-Star Team. (Ronnie Peach.)

JOHNNY NEWMAN AND VINCENT MULLEN. Here are Owensboro Oilers outfielder Johnny Newman (left) and Jackson Generals second baseman-manager Vincent "Moon" Mullen at Miller Field in 1939. That season, Newman set the Kitty League single-season record with 33 home runs. Mullen, a .309 hitter in six seasons with the Mayfield Clothiers, Jackson, and Fulton Tigers, batted .292 and led the Generals to a fourth-place finish. (Cam Mullen-Oates.)

HARRY GRISWOLD. A right hand–hitting catcher, Griswold batted .293 with 67 RBIs as player-manager of the Hopkinsville Hoppers and was named to the Kitty League All-Star team. Despite a lineup with two of the best hitters in the league—Stanley Stencel (.359, 118 RBIs) and Carl Alto (.347, 21 triples)—Hopkinsville finished the season in fourth place, 19 games behind the league champion Mayfield Browns.

1940 BOWLING GREEN BARONS. The Lexington (Tennessee) Bees franchise moved to Bowling Green, Kentucky, in 1939, and for four seasons the Barons played at Fairgrounds Park on Lehman Avenue. A year later, they won their only Kitty League pennant, led by manager Ellis "Mike" Powers (front row, fourth from left). Joe Lehan (front row, third from left) batted .359 with 45 doubles and 95 RBIs, Lloyd Heitman (front row, far left) hit 11 home runs with 76 RBIs, and Bernard Kincannon (back row, fifth from left) won 15 games. Bowling Green won the second-half title, and despite losing the split-season playoff to the Jackson Generals, the Barons' overall record earned them the pennant. In this photograph, notice that some players still have the baseball centennial patches on their sleeves from the previous season. (Arleen Ireland.)

LEFTY HAAS. A three-time 20-game winner in the Kitty League, Elmer Haas compiled an impressive 80-35 record and 2.91 ERA in four seasons with the Hopkinsville Hoppers and Bowling Green Barons. In 1939, he tied the single-season record of 25 wins held by Hub Perdue of the 1906 Vincennes Alices, winning 10 straight games to reach the mark. Haas's baseball career ended prematurely at the age of 27 when he contracted infantile paralysis (or polio) following the 1941 season. He was inducted into the Kitty League Hall of Fame in 2003. (Arleen Ireland.)

1940 PADUCAH INDIANS. Managed by Innes "Rip" Fanning (second row, second from right), the Indians finished in second place in both halves of the split-season standings behind the Jackson Generals and Bowling Green Barons. Leon Balser led the pitching staff with 22 victories and Dave Koslo with 246 strikeouts. Outfielder Roy Bueschen batted .347 with 46 doubles, 94 RBIs, and 101 runs scored.

UNIQUE AUTOGRAPH. In addition to the signatures of manager Rip Fanning and all-star Clint Andereck, this 1940 Paducah Indians baseball bears the distinctive autograph of pitcher Leon Balser, who won 22 games for Paducah and was named to the Kitty League All-Star Team in 1940. Tragically, he was killed seven years later in a railroad accident while working as a switchman during the off-season in Cleveland; he was 29 years old.

OPENING DAY AT MILLER FIELD. A marching band and military review highlighted the festivities in Owensboro, Kentucky, on May 8, 1940. In a season that averaged 12.6 runs scored per game throughout the league, the Oilers hit .303 as a team in 1940. Three-fourths of the all-star infield were Oilers: batting champion Frank McElyea (.400, 49 doubles, 108 RBIs), Don DeVault (.357), and Leonard Novak (.316, 70 RBIs). (Ronnie Peach.)

EDDIE URBON. The Owensboro outfielder set a new league record with 34 home runs in 1940, exceeding the mark set by former teammate Johnny Newman a year earlier. On the last day of the season, September 8, 1940, Urbon hit two homers at Miller Field to tie and break the record. He batted .332 with 66 home runs and 214 RBIs in three seasons from 1939 to 1941. (Ronnie Peach.)

1940 JACKSON GENERALS. The Generals won the first-half title and beat the Bowling Green Barons in the split-season playoff. The men pictured are, from left to right, (first row) manager Mickey O'Neil, Ernest Ankrom, Mel Merkel, Joe Polcha, Dick Jones, Earl Griffin, and Harry Williams; (second row) club president Hartle Gilliand, Charles Martin, Al Cuozzo, Ellis Kinder, Newt "Gashouse" Parker, Charley Graves, Carl Gaiser, Mel Reist, and club vice president Shaler "Preacher" Gilliand. (Fred Baker.)

ELLIS KINDER. The Arkansas native won 21 games for the Jackson Generals, led the league with a 2.38 ERA, and set a new Kitty League record with 307 strikeouts in 276 innings pitched. Nicknamed "Old Folks" during his 12-year major-league career, he won 23 games as a starter for the Boston Red Sox in 1949 and became a successful relief pitcher later in his career.

THE PRIDE OF MEDINA. Jesse Webb, the laid-back pitcher with the sweeping roundhouse curve from Medina, Tennessee, won 131 games and struck out 1,611 batters in eight seasons with the Jackson Generals from 1935 to 1942 and one with the Union City Greyhounds in 1946. In 1941, he had 25 wins and 248 strikeouts. Webb was elected to the Kitty League Hall of Fame in 1953. (Bernice Webb Thompson.)

ELLIS "MIKE" POWERS. The former big-league outfielder finished second in the batting race at .380 as player-manager for the Bowling Green Barons in 1940. His 155 RBIs were a single-season record that stood for 14 years. Powers had played two seasons for the Cleveland Indians in 1932 and 1933. (Arleen Ireland.)

1940 MAYFIELD BROWNS. The Browns tied for fifth place in the first half of the season and finished fourth in the second half. Pictured are, from left to right, (first row) Joe Rayne, Norman Litzinger, Lloyd Patterson, manager Benny Tate, Marion DeJarnett, Marcus Carrola, and Richard Kimble; (second row) Ed Lanfersieck, John Nolan, Marlin Stuart, George Bender Jr., bus driver Leonard Nall, club president Doyle Hutchinson, Tom Tucker, John Gotter, Bob White, and Mike Kowal.

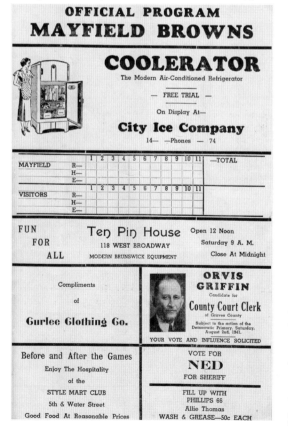

1940 MAYFIELD BROWNS SCORECARD. It was obviously an election year in Graves County, Kentucky, based on advertisements paid for on this scorecard. One candidate thought he was so well known that his front-page ad simply read, "Vote for Ned for Sheriff." This scorecard was sold to fans at Hunt Park, home of the Clothiers and Browns from 1937 to 1941. The team's board of directors purchased the ballpark for $3,750.

BILLY GOFF AND DUTCH WELCH. Local wrestling promoter Billy Goff (left) was named general manager of the Hopkinsville Hoppers in 1940. He later became team owner from 1946 to 1952 and built Kentucky Park, the Hoppers' post–World War II ballpark. Hopkinsville finished in last place under new manager Herbert "Dutch" Welch (right), whose five-year Kitty League managerial record from 1935 to 1940 ended at 230-245. (William Turner collection.)

ROGER WRIGHT AND JAMES BRYAN. This photograph was taken at Mercer Park in Hopkinsville, Kentucky, in 1940. Wright (left) pitched for the Bowling Green Barons and Hopkinsville Hoppers and had a 3.94 ERA despite a 5-12 record. Bryan hit .339 with 41 RBIs in 46 games. (Lewis "Shine" Richardson.)

DAVE KOSLO. The Menasha, Wisconsin, native had an 11-14 record and 194 strikeouts for the Hopkinsville Hoppers in 1939. A year later, he won 17 games and struck out 246 batters for the Paducah Indians. Koslo pitched 12 seasons in the major leagues with the New York Giants, Baltimore Orioles, and Milwaukee Braves from 1941 to 1955. He was inducted into the Kitty League Hall of Fame in 1953.

RAY CLONTS. A catcher for the Fulton Eagles/Tigers, Cairo Egyptians, and Union City Greyhounds from 1936 to 1947, the Douglasville, Georgia, native batted .284 with 330 RBIs in 508 games. Clonts also managed Fulton in 1938 and Cairo in 1947. His best season was 1939 when he hit .310 and drove in 80 runs for sixth-place Fulton and—as many Kitty League players did—married a local girl, Mary Elizabeth Powers. (Dianne Cundiff.)

UMPIRE-IN-CHIEF. Ellis Beggs endured 12 seasons of verbal and physical abuse as a Kitty League umpire from 1938 to 1950. One memorable game went 20 innings between the Fulton Eagles and Paducah Indians on July 8 and 9, 1938. It lasted five hours and 28 minutes and ended at 1:45 a.m. Beggs was named the league's umpire-in-chief in 1946. He was inducted into the Kitty League Hall of Fame in 2005. (Elaine Forrester.)

1940 SEASON PASS. This pass allowed umpire Ellis Beggs and his wife free admission to all Kitty League games. It was signed by Pres. Ben F. Howard, a Union City, Tennessee, resident who guided the circuit in 1939 and 1940. (Elaine Forrester.)

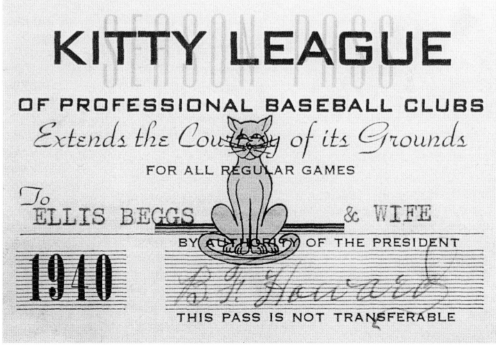

SEASON PASS

KITTY LEAGUE
OF PROFESSIONAL BASEBALL CLUBS
Extends the Courtesy of its Grounds
FOR ALL REGULAR GAMES

To
ELLIS BEGGS   & WIFE

BY AUTHORITY OF THE PRESIDENT

1940   *B. F. Howard*

THIS PASS IS NOT TRANSFERABLE

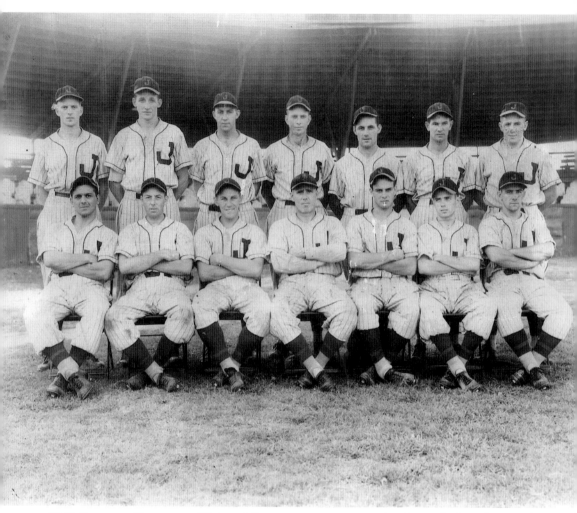

1941 Jackson Generals. With a .661 winning percentage, the Generals (84-43) were the greatest Kitty League team prior to World War II. They captured the pennant in dominating fashion with a 14.5-game lead over their nearest rival, combining great pitching by two 20-game winners (Carl Gaiser, who set a new league record with 26, and Jesse Webb, who won 25) with booming bats that hit a league-leading 114 home runs. (First baseman Mel Merkel led the league with 30.) Before his promotion to Class C ball, William Newton "Gashouse" Parker belted 16 homers in the first 20 games of the season. Pictured are, from left to right, (first row) Al Cuozzo, Jesse Webb, Ernie Ankrom, manager Mickey O'Neil, Lynn Hornsby, Ray Haynes, and Lloyd Maloney; (second row) Andy Scarbola, Charley Graves, Carl Gaiser, Ellis Kinder, Wallace Noon, Mel Reist, and Mel Merkel. (Albert Merkel.)

KITTY LEAGUE MATCHBOOK. Among league president Ben F. Howard's promotional ideas in 1940 was this red and blue matchbook with silver border. Inside is a list of all eight league towns and their respective club presidents.

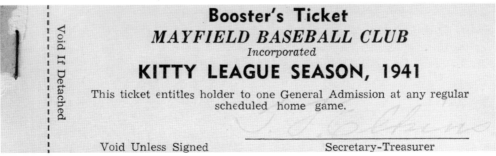

Booster's Ticket
MAYFIELD BASEBALL CLUB
Incorporated
KITTY LEAGUE SEASON, 1941
This ticket entitles holder to one General Admission at any regular scheduled home game.

Void Unless Signed   Secretary-Treasurer

Void If Detached

1941 MAYFIELD BROWNS BOOSTER TICKETS. The Browns created a ticket and promotion committee comprised of T.T. Elkins, Ray Kiesey, and Hoyt Weaver to sell stapled books of booster tickets for the 1941 season. Elkin's stamped signature as secretary-treasurer of the ballclub is affixed to each ticket.

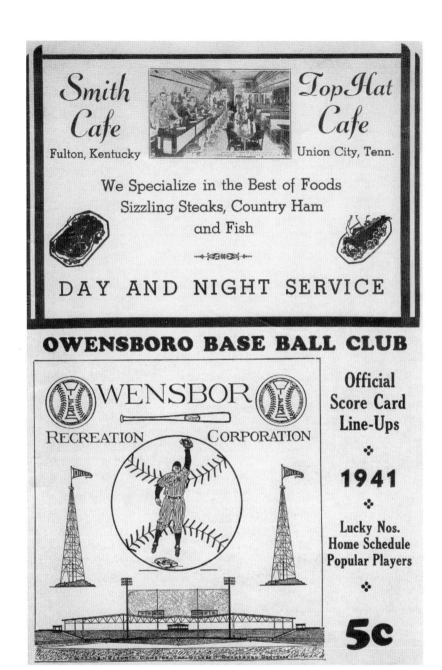

1941 Owensboro Oilers Scorecard. The detailed illustration of the Miller Field grandstand makes this an attractive scorecard. It is also unique for two additional reasons: it features an out-of-town advertiser on the front cover (the Smith Café was a popular hangout for players in Fulton), and inside the scorecard is a list of hotels where the Oilers stayed on the road. Because Owensboro was the furthest town in the circuit, overnight stays for the team was a necessity. The hotels where they stayed in 1941 were the Helm Hotel in Bowling Green, the Usona Hotel in Fulton, the New Southern Hotel in Jackson, the Hall Hotel in Mayfield, the Ritz Hotel in Paducah, and the Davy Crockett Hotel in Union City.

1941 OWENSBORO OILERS PITCHERS. From left to right are Tommy Combs, Eddie Haushild, Alex Heath, Arnold Heft, Bobby Foster, and Tommy Keeton. Combs had a 1-0 record and 3.27 ERA in 12 games. Hauschild pitched in 16 games (1-0, 2.49 ERA) and played 33 games at third base, batting .255 with two home runs and 21 RBIs. Heath won 14 games with a 3.77 ERA. Heft led the league with 264 strikeouts and was the best hitting pitcher on the staff with a .259 average and 14 RBIs. Foster had a 4-9 record and 5.56 ERA. Keeton was 11-16 with 166 strikeouts. (Ronnie Peach.)

GEORGE WILSON AND WALLY SCHANG. The 16-year-old rookie George Wilson batted .316 with 33 RBIs in 48 games for Owensboro in the abbreviated 1942 season. Here, he poses with Oilers manager and former big-league catcher Wally Schang, who played 19 seasons, mostly with the Philadelphia Athletics, Boston Red Sox, and New York Yankees, from 1913 to 1931. (Ronnie Peach.)

SAM DENTE AND JOE SCOTT. Owensboro teammates Sam Dente (on the ground) and Joe Scott horse around at Miller Field in 1941. Dente was a shortstop who batted .273 in 77 games and would play six major-league seasons, mostly with the Washington Senators and Cleveland Indians, from 1947 to 1955. Scott played in 101 games at first base for the Oilers and hit .262 with 43 RBIs. (Ronnie Peach.)

ARNOLD HEFT. Heft won 22 games with a league-best 264 strikeouts and 2.42 ERA for Owensboro in 1941. When his baseball career ended, he became one of the first referees for the Basketball Association of America—now known as the NBA—and officiated from 1946 to 1961. He and his partners purchased the Baltimore Bullets in 1963, which later became the Washington Bullets (now the Wizards). (Arnold Heft.)

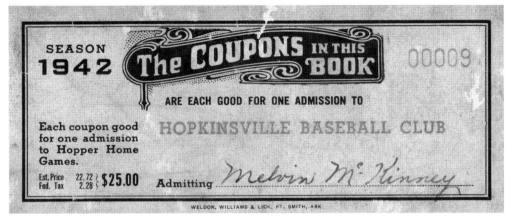

1942 HOPKINSVILLE HOPPERS SEASON TICKET BOOK. The Hoppers went forward despite warnings of potential hardship by league president Shelby Peace if the teams wanted to play ball in 1942. America had entered World War II, and young ballplayers were being drafted into military service. The league eventually disbanded on June 19 with the Fulton Tigers in first place. The Hoppers finished in fourth place at 23-23. (William Turner collection.)

1942 OWENSBORO OILERS PLAYERS. From left to right are Ivan Kuester, Ray Rieber, Hubert Wilson, and Tex DeMasters. In his second season with Owensboro, Kuester hit .311 in 20 games. Rieber had a 3-4 record and 3.82 ERA, and DeMasters was 4-6 with 65 strikeouts and a 2.92 ERA. Wilson had a brief stint with the Oilers. (Ronnie Peach.)

THE "LITTLE SECOND BASEMAN." That is how the Union City sportswriter described 19-year-old Albert "Red" Schoendienst, who made his professional debut with the Greyhounds at Bowling Green, Kentucky, on June 12, 1942. Batting sixth in the lineup, he went three for five with a double and an RBI, turned his first double play, and committed his first error. Schoendienst batted .407 in six games (only one of which was played in Union City on June 16) before the Kitty League folded on June 18. In 1953, he was inducted into the league's hall of fame, a choice undoubtedly based more on his 19-year major-league career than his brief stint in the league. The former St. Louis Cardinals, New York Giants, and Milwaukee Braves player was elected to the Baseball Hall of Fame in 1989. (National Baseball Hall of Fame Library.)

STRIKE THREE

PROSPERITY AND DEMISE, 1946–1955

The Kitty League emerged from its wartime slumber in 1946 with Shelby Peace back at the helm. For the first time since 1924, it was truly the Kitty League with teams in Kentucky (Fulton, Hopkinsville, Madisonville, Mayfield, and Owensboro), Illinois (Cairo), and Tennessee (Clarksville and Union City). Minor-league baseball enjoyed renewed popularity in the postwar years, and the Kitty League enjoyed its longest and most successful run of 10 seasons between 1946 and 1955. It boasted attendance figures of 350,000 or more in 1947 and 1948, led by the Owensboro Oilers, pennant winners in three out of four seasons. Whereas the largest city in the league had the best teams in the 1940s, the next decade was dominated by one of the smallest towns in organized baseball. The Railroaders and Lookouts of Fulton, Kentucky (population over 3,000), won three consecutive pennants in 1951, 1952, and 1953, and averaged over 29,000 fans each season. During this postwar period, 17 future major leaguers played in the league.

Air-conditioned homes, drive-in movie theaters, and radio and television broadcasts of major-league games in the 1950s led fewer and fewer fans to Kitty League ballparks. Attendance was cut in half during its final season in 1955, falling from 241,266 in 1954 to 120,187 a year later, a far cry from the 361,085 figure in 1946. Its demise began in 1954 with a historic 27-game losing streak by the Jackson Generals. The day after the streak ended so did the Generals, and the franchise finished the season in Central City, Kentucky. The Hopkinsville Hoppers, who had played in all but two seasons of the league's existence, did not return in 1955. Even though the Madisonville Miners had folded on July 7, 1955, the league hobbled through until September with five clubs and no postseason playoffs in its final season. With the Kitty League, there was always hope for another life. Hope ended, however, with the death of its longtime stalwart Shelby Peace in 1958.

1946 OWENSBORO OILERS. This photograph was taken in front of the home dugout at Miller Field. From left to right are Wilson Musgraves, Dick Fischer, Chuck Tanner, Bill Richards, Joe Matosky, Hank Martyniak, Jim Keller, Bill McGee, Dick Weitelman, Wally Buerger, George Buickel, Earl Browne, Ray Fletcher, Dale Leeper, F.M. Younger, and batboy Jackie Akers. The 1946 Oilers were second only to the 1952 Fulton Lookouts with the highest winning percentage in league history at .680. They captured the pennant with a record of 83-39, finishing 12 games ahead of their nearest rival, and won the postseason Shaughnessy playoffs as well. It was the best hitting team with a league-leading .308 batting average. Among their three 100-RBI batters was third baseman Walter Buerger, who hit .346 with 17 home runs and 113 RBIs. (Hank Martyniak.)

EARL BROWNE. "Snitz" was a 17-year minor-league veteran when he came to Owensboro in 1946. He spent four seasons in the major leagues with the Pittsburgh Pirates and Philadelphia Phillies from 1935 to 1938. In 1946 and 1947, Browne batted .427 with 28 home runs and 193 RBIs in 199 games and led the Oilers to two straight pennants. He was elected to the Kitty League Hall of Fame in 2005. (Ronnie Peach.)

SILVER SLUGGER. The only batter in Kitty League history to hit over .400 in two seasons, Earl Browne led all of professional baseball—minors and majors—with a .429 batting average in 1946. The 35-year-old Louisville native was presented with a silver Louisville Slugger bat by the Hillerich and Bradsby Company during a ceremony at Miller Field on June 17, 1947. Among other gifts he received from appreciative fans was a brand new automobile. He told them, "Well, when I'm riding around town and you see me, stop me and get in." (David Kitterman.)

RAY FLETCHER. The 21-year-old New York City native batted .341 with a league-leading 32 home runs and 140 RBIs for Owensboro in 1946; he also had 32 doubles and scored 126 runs. On May 23, 1946, Fletcher collected seven RBIs in a game against the Cairo Egyptians. (Ronnie Peach.)

1946 HOPKINSVILLE HOPPERS. Managed by 35-year-old minor-league veteran Calvin Chapman, the Hoppers finished in second place with a 73-53 record. Chapman batted .380 with 19 home runs in 72 games. Rookie Harold "Buster" Boguskie led the team with his league-leading 190 hits and .355 batting average. Floyd Fogg contributed 21 home runs and 96 RBIs. Pete Rhodes won 16 games with a 3.13 ERA. (William Turner collection.)

JOHN MCPHERSON. The left-hand hitting outfielder played two seasons for Hopkinsville in 1946 and 1948, batting .322 with 192 RBIs in 213 games. Here, he sits with a group of fans at Hopkinsville's Kentucky Park in 1946. (William Turner collection.)

1946 FULTON CHICKS. A farm club of the Memphis Chicks in the Southern Association, the third-place Fulton club (69-56) beat the Hopkinsville Hoppers in the first round of the Shaughnessy playoffs and battled the league champion Owensboro Oilers in seven games. The players appear to be wearing former Detroit Tigers uniforms left over from the 1942 Fulton team. (Carolyn Peterson Thornberry.)

BOB SCHULTZ. The 23-year-old rookie had a 19-10 record and 3.62 ERA with Fulton in 1946. Schultz shattered the Kitty League single-season record with 361 strikeouts in 221 innings pitched. He struck out 21 Madisonville Miners batters on June 29 and threw a seven-inning no-hitter against the Union City Greyhounds on August 21. Schultz pitched for the Chicago Cubs, Pittsburgh Pirates, and Detroit Tigers from 1951 to 1955. (Skip Nipper.)

CARROLL "PETE" PETERSON. An outfielder from Columbia, South Carolina, Peterson batted .274 with 23 doubles and 80 RBIs for Fulton in 1946. He played eight seasons with Fulton and Mayfield from 1940 to 1951 and hit .306 with 805 hits, 47 home runs, and 509 RBIs in 676 games. He was inducted into the Kitty League Hall of Fame in 2003. (Carolyn Peterson Thornberry.)

HAL SEAWRIGHT. The Fulton outfielder and third baseman was the team's leading hitter in 1946, batting .355 with 23 home runs, 122 RBIs, and 101 runs scored. A Cairo, Illinois, native, Seawright played five seasons for Fulton, Cairo, Jackson, and Hopkinsville with an overall .327 batting average, 77 homers, and 538 RBIs in 559 games. He was inducted into the Kitty League Hall of Fame in 2003. (Betty Seawright.)

1946 MADISONVILLE MINERS SCORECARD. Madisonville, Kentucky, returned to the Kitty League for the first time since 1922. If the announcer at Municipal Park had called out lucky No. 1471, the owner of this scorecard would have won two free tickets. An advertisement for Sharp's Bakery asked fans to "Make Home Run Hitters Out of Your Youngsters by Giving Them Plenty of Cakes, Cookies, and Donuts! Good for Grown-Ups Too!"

HOMER JOHNSTON. The left-hand hitting first baseman batted .353 in 204 games for the Union City Greyhounds in 1940 and 1941 and the Cairo Egyptians in 1946. Before his contract was sold to the Class B Waterloo, Iowa, club in August 1946, Johnston's .453 average in 64 games was the highest nominal batting average in league history. This photograph was taken at Egyptian Field in Cairo, Illinois. (Karen Johnston Staten.)

1946 Union City Greyhounds. The seventh-place Greyhounds were managed by former big-leaguer Johnny Gill, who hit .378 with 17 home runs and 83 RBIs in 71 games. Milton Sidewell was the league leader in being hit by 25 pitches. Howard Bentz led the pitching staff with his 14-14 record and 3.62 ERA. Kitty League veteran 36-year-old Jesse Webb contributed a 6-5 record and 3.73 ERA. (Bernice Webb Thompson.)

Union City Greyhounds Players. From left to right are third baseman Danny Verderbar, outfielder Robert Sepanek, and catcher Martin Zuba. Verderbar batted .290 with 12 home runs and 74 RBIs, Sepanek hit .236 with 33 RBIs, and Zuba hit .251 with 42 RBIs. (Ruth Neuman Carver.)

HAPPY OCCASION. Baseball commissioner Albert B. "Happy" Chandler attended a game at Mayfield, Kentucky, between the Clothiers and Fulton Chicks on August 19, 1946. As a boy, the former Kentucky governor and U.S. senator remembered chasing foul balls at the Kitty League ballpark in Henderson. Here he poses with Fulton manager Hugh Holliday (left) and Mayfield skipper Eddie O'Connell.

Souvenier Program

opening game of the

Kitty League Season

Hopkinsville Hoppers
vs
Clarksville Owls

Tuesday Night, May 7, 1946

sponsored by the

Veterans of Foreign Wars
Howard (Smiley) Johnson Post

Support Our Team
LET'S GO OWLS!

1946 CLARKSVILLE OWLS SCORECARD. Clarksville, Tennessee, had not hosted a Kitty League club since 1916. The Owls played at Goodrich Field, a converted softball field located adjacent to the B.F. Goodrich Rubber Company plant. It was a bandbox ballpark known for its short fences. One out-of-town sportswriter remarked that the only way to hit a triple was to "knock the ball over the fence and stop on third base."

LEAGUE CONSTITUTION AND BYLAWS. This booklet governed the Kitty League for the 1947 season. One unusual rule did not allow radio broadcasters to "second-guess plays, suggest how the play should have been executed," or "criticize the players, managers, club or umpires for the way in which they perform their duties." The league president could cancel contracts between the team and radio station if the rule was violated.

1947 KITTY LEAGUE MILEAGE CHART. Each club tried to avoid the expense of overnight stays whenever possible. For teams within close proximity such as Fulton and Union City and Clarksville and Hopkinsville, it was easy to commute back and forth. Because Owensboro was the furthest club in the loop, most teams had no choice but to rent rooms at the Hotel Owensboro or the Rudd Hotel. (William Turner collection.)

OFFICIAL
CONSTITUTION AND BY-LAWS

OF THE

KITTY LEAGUE

CLASS D

Member National Association of Professional
Baseball Leagues

SHELBY PEACE, President .... Hopkinsville, Ky.
ALLEN CLOAR, Vice-President .... Mayfield, Ky.
VERA FUQUA, Secretary .... Hopkinsville, Ky.
MAYO FERGUSON, Treasurer......Hopkinsville, Ky.
J. P. FRIEND, Statistician .... Blythesville, Ark.

KITTY LEAGUE MILEAGE CHART

U. S. TIRES — BATTERIES
MADISONVILLE RECAPPING COMPANY
The Best In Service and Satisfaction
Telephone 157
FEDERAL STREET - OPPOSITE P. O.

	UNION CITY	FULTON	MAYFIELD	CAIRO	CLARKSVILLE	HOPKINSVILLE	MADISONVILLE	OWENSBORO
UNION CITY		12	35	57	106	104	139	188
FULTON	12		23	45	106	92	127	174
MAYFIELD	35	23		45	94	69	104	153
CAIRO	57	45	45		139	114	122	164
CLARKSVILLE	106	106	94	139		25	60	109
HOPKINSVILLE	104	92	69	114	25		35	84
MADISONVILLE	139	127	104	122	60	35		49
OWENSBORO	188	174	153	164	109	84	49	

EARL BROWNE. In this photograph, the Owensboro first baseman-manager scoops a ball out of the dirt at Miller Field. Browne hit .425 in 107 games with fewer home runs than the previous season (7) but drove in 93 runs. He guided the Oilers to their second straight pennant in 1947 with a record of 77-48, though they were eliminated in the playoffs by the Hopkinsville Hoppers. (Ronnie Peach.)

1947 MAYFIELD CLOTHIERS. The second-place Clothiers finished 4.5 games behind Owensboro. Pictured are, from left to right, (first row) John Howson, Noble Bell, Melvin Held, Alfred DeMarcantonio, Joe Dworak, Norman Arant, Guy Brill, Bill Bordt, and groundskeeper Albert Austin; (second row) business manager Acree Austin, manager Shan Deniston, Robert Mainzer, Eddie Rzendzian, Harold Bollinger, Edward Palko, Lawson Williams Jr., Paul Zubak, Tommy Bergdoll, John Conner, club treasurer William T. Gibson, and bus driver Bill Coleman; Bobby Allen is batboy.

1947 HOPKINSVILLE HOPPERS. The third-place Hoppers beat Owensboro in the first round and Madisonville in the finals to win the playoff title. Pictured are, from left to right, (first row) Bob Stapenhoerst, Joe Richardson, Al Chapman, Charles Oubre, Newt Secrest, John Kall, Frank Scalzi, and Paul Stack; (second row) Paul McGlothin, Ron Ham, Bob Foster, George Reding, John Gamble, James "Dusty" Rhodes, Ray Bowers, Jim Atchley, Billy Forbes, and owner Billy Goff. (William Turner collection.)

DUSTY RHODES AND SHELBY PEACE. James "Dusty" Rhodes played for Hopkinsville in 1947 and batted .326 with 12 home runs and 92 RBIs. With the New York and San Francisco Giants from 1952 to 1959, his clutch hits in the 1954 World Series earned him folk hero status. That winter, he was honored at a banquet in Hopkinsville and received a wristwatch from Kitty League president Shelby Peace.

1947 MADISONVILLE MINERS SCORECARD. The Chicago White Sox farm club finished in fourth place and earned a playoff spot but lost to Hopkinsville in the finals. Robert Proulx hit .359 with 126 runs scored. Richard Szpond led the league with 128 RBIs. Future big-leaguer Herb Adams batted .405 in 54 games and played for the White Sox the following season. (William Turner collection.)

BOB BUHL. The Chicago White Sox signed the 18-year-old high school pitcher and assigned him to Madisonville in 1947. There, he had a 19-10 record and 3.00 ERA with 185 strikeouts. Because Chicago signed him before he actually received his diploma, Buhl became a free agent and signed with the Boston Braves. He pitched 15 seasons in the major leagues, most with the Milwaukee Braves, from 1953 to 1967.

1947 CAIRO EGYPTIANS. The Egyptians finished in sixth place. Kenneth Hahn hit .312 and broke the league record with 55 stolen bases. Pictured are, from left to right, (front row) John Mathes, Jerry Burns, Leo Corley, Bob Crain, Jim Sweet, Gene Moore, and Olen "Jack" Bridges; (back row) manager Orace "Pudge" Powers, Delbert Britt, David Thieke, Bill Holt, Jim Liming, Walter Lindsey, Buck Driskell, Kenneth Hahn, and John Hobbs; ? Sullivan is the batboy.

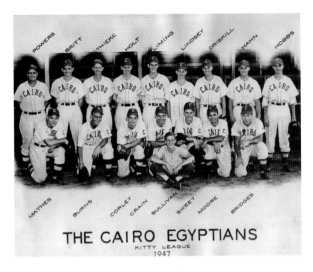

1948 UNION CITY GREYHOUNDS. The second-place Greyhounds took four straight from Madisonville to win the playoff title. Pictured are, from left to right, (first row) manager George "Tony" Rensa, Eulas "Bud" Hutson, Jacque Riedel, Bob Samaras, and Harold "Bud" Pfeiffer; (second row) Kenny Paulus, Joe Linn, Carl "Corky" Bellers, Gil Wick, Don Petschow, and Les Filkins; (third row) Clarence "Dutch" Neuman, Charlie Simpson, Herm Wollitz, LeRoy Fisher, and Bernie Olinger. (Ruth Neuman Carver.)

1948 HOPKINSVILLE HOPPERS. The pennant-winning Hoppers (85-41) finished with a .675 winning percentage, third-best in Kitty League history. Thirty-six-year-old Vito Tamulis, who pitched six seasons in the major leagues, won 17 games with 205 strikeouts and a league-leading 2.32 ERA. At the plate, he hit .355 with five homers and 35 RBIs. John Mueller, whose .353 average was third in the league, scored 115 runs and drove in 124 while stealing 36 bases. Second baseman John Kall led the league with 23 home runs and 139 runs scored. The team failed to advance in the Shaughnessy playoffs, however, losing to the Madisonville Miners three games to two. The men pictured are, from left to right, (first row) George Reding, Al Chapman, Leo Blandino, Frank Hughes, Hal Marak, Al Ketchum, Marion Hill, Newt Secrest, and John Trammel; (second row) manager Vito Tamulis, John Kall, Jim Liming, Roy Bowers, John McPherson, John Mueller, Billy Forbes, and Joe Bohl. (William Turner collection.)

1948 Cairo Egyptians Scorecard. The Egyptians finished in seventh place under managers Hugh Holliday and Norbert Hall. Lester Severin won the league batting title with a .381 average and 118 RBIs. Joe Riolo batted .352 with 103 RBIs. Norbert Habel led the pitching staff with a 9-8 record.

Official
KITTY LEAGUE
DIRECTORY

1948

Kitty League Directory. This two-sided pamphlet gave information about the league in 1948 with lists of league and club officers and umpires and a game schedule. League officers were Pres. Shelby Peace, Vice Pres. Allen Cloar, secretary Vera Fuqua, treasurer Mayo Ferguson, and statistician J.P. Friend. Frank Cayce Company, a men's clothing-store and sporting-goods supplier in Hopkinsville, Kentucky, was the official distributor of league baseballs. (William Turner collection.)

HOPKINSVILLE HOPPERS PENCIL SCHEDULE. The Hoppers created this functional item to let fans know when the team would be playing at Kentucky Park in 1948. (William Turner collection.)

1949 OWENSBORO OILERS SCORECARD. A favorite design for the Oilers, it often appeared on scorecards from this period. The team captured its third league pennant in four seasons under manager Marion "Bill" Adair, who contributed a league-leading 23 home runs. Its .672 winning percentage was the fourth best in league history. Don Hazelton set a new single-season record with 84 stolen bases while scoring a league-best 116 runs. (Ronnie Peach.)

RAY CRONE. The 17-year-old right-hander from Memphis, Tennessee, won nine games and struck out 102 batters in 89 innings for Owensboro in his first professional season in 1949. He was named to the Kitty League All-Star Team. Crone went on to pitch five seasons for the Milwaukee Braves, New York Giants, and San Francisco Giants from 1954 to 1958. (Earl Hamann.)

RAY CATTANEO. A slick-fielding third baseman, Cattaneo hit .308 with 15 home runs and 102 RBIs for Owensboro in 1949 and was named to the Kitty League All-Star Team. This photograph shows him in the visitor's on-deck circle at Municipal Stadium in Madisonville, Kentucky. (Earl Hamann.)

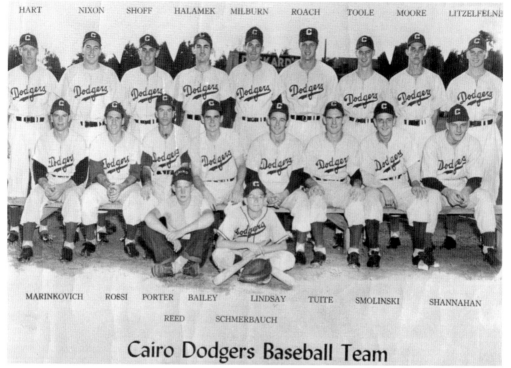

HART   NIXON   SHOFF   HALAMEK   MILBURN   ROACH   TOOLE   MOORE   LITZELFELNE

MARINKOVICH   ROSSI   PORTER   BAILEY   LINDSAY   TUITE   SMOLINSKI   SHANNAHAN

REED   SCHMERBAUCH

Cairo Dodgers Baseball Team

1949 CAIRO DODGERS. Manager and former major leaguer Bill Hart won the batting title with a .404 average. The second-place Dodgers made it into the playoff finals against Madisonville. Pictured are, from left to right, (first row) Frank Marinkovich, Marion Rossi, Elwood Porter, Leonard Bailey, Walter Lindsay, Leo Tuite, Carl Smolinski, and Jack Shannahan; (second row) manager Bill Hart, Jack Nixon, Willis Shoff, Louis Halamek, Morris Milburn, Gordon Roach, Robert Toole, Lloyd Moore, and Jack Litzelfelner; the batboys are Bob Reed and Bobby Schmerbauch.

1949 HOPKINSVILLE HOPPERS. John Mueller (front row, third from left) took over as player-manager in 1949 and had an all-star season, batting .373 with 97 RBIs and 97 runs scored. Joe Podoley hit .323 with 12 home runs and 83 RBIs, and pitcher Ned Thaxton won 15 games. The third-place Hoppers (68-56) qualified for the Shaughnessy playoffs but lost in the first round to the Cairo Dodgers. (William Turner collection.)

1949 HOPKINSVILLE HOPPERS SCORECARD. Concession prices at Kentucky Park were 10¢ for this scorecard, 15¢ for a hot dog, 10¢ for a bag of peanuts, 25¢ for a soft drink, and 20¢ for a beer or 25¢ for a premium beer. Frank Cayce Company advertised itself as the downtown ticket office for the Hoppers, and the New Central Hotel was where the visiting teams stayed. Young Hardware Company in Hopkinsville was the local dealer for the McGregor-Goldsmith official league baseball. WHOP (still broadcasting today) carried the Hoppers' home and road games. Although Kitty League founder Dr. Frank H. Bassett did not attend their games, he still supported the Hoppers and placed his own advertisement. It read, "For 46 years the friend of the Kitty / For 28 years your County Court Clerk / For 75 years everybody's friend / Nuff said. / Dr. Frank H. Bassett."

1949 FULTON RAILROADERS. The Railroaders finished in sixth place. Pictured are, from left to right, (first row) an unidentified batboy, Bill Bishop, John Bohna, Perry "Tex" Brown, and Carl Ashford; (second row) Charley Tate, Harley Grossman, Ralph "Chicken" Brawner, Curt Englebright, Ralph Fraser, Ned Waldrop, and Toby Fisher; (third row) Carroll "Pete" Peterson, manager Ivan Kuester, Bob Coker, Andy Collins, Ralph "Red" Bickering, Wilford "Junior" Cunningham, and Mike Conovan. (Dr. Curtis L. Englebright.)

FULTON RAILROADERS BUS. Fulton players derisively called their team bus the "Blue Goose." Pitcher Wilford "Junior" Cunningham received extra pay to be the driver. Unlike school buses that many teams employed, the Railroaders had a converted city bus with high-backed seats for better comfort. But it became notorious in 1949 for failing brakes, wires catching fire, and a broken tie-rod. (Dr. Curtis L. Englebright.)

OLD RELIABLE. Curt Englebright played six seasons for Cairo, Hopkinsville, Fulton, and Union City from 1947 to 1952. When he was traded from Hopkinsville to Fulton in 1948, Hoppers owner Billy Goff and Fulton team representative Hillard H. Bugg negotiated the deal in the lobby of a Union City, Tennessee, hotel where the team was staying overnight. With an agreement reached, Englebright met with Goff to receive his final salary payment. Payday had been a few days earlier and after deducting an advance, Goff owed Englebright $9.33 and wrote him a check. A young woman who had overheard the earlier negotiations stopped him. "You ought to be ashamed of yourself," she told Goff. He asked why and she replied, "For selling a cute boy like that for $9.33." (Dr. Curtis L. Englebright.)

1949 UNION CITY GREYHOUNDS. The Greyhounds finished in fifth place. Pictured are, from left to right, (first row) batboys Freddie Palmer and Paul Strickland; (second row) Louie Perego, John "Jabby" Ellison, Carl "Corky" Bellers, George Martak, and Jim Dambach; (third row) Dominic "Dom" Serefini, Joe Linn, Bob Leonhard, Billy Joe Forrest, Jim Jadwin, and Jim Morris; (fourth row) Shelby "Red" Kincaid, Dick Dutton, manager Rudy York, Lee Aldridge, Bernie Olinger, and Bill McDonald.

1949 CLARKSVILLE COLTS. In their last season, the Colts finished in seventh place. All-star Maurice Partain stole 50 bases, and Dick Janasky won 14 games. Pictured are, from left to right, (first row) Clyde Englebright, Walt Mestan, Hod Lisenbee, Dick Janasky, and Hayden Ray; (second row) Norman Hammons, Don Stevens, Leonard Addison, Bill Hedges, Andy Sventko, and Jack Finch; (third row) Jim Troop, Lee Valadez, Bob Swope, Doyle Pruett, Jack Spiceland, and Maurice Partain. (Walt Mestan.)

1949 CLARKSVILLE COLTS SCORECARD. Originally called the Owls when Clarksville returned to the Kitty League in 1946, the Colts had finished in the second division for the past four seasons. One highlight was second baseman Billy Herman Jr., son of the Chicago Cubs Hall of Fame infielder, starting triple plays in two consecutive games on May 4 and 5, 1949, before his eventual release.

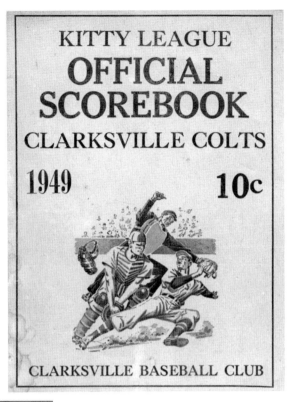

KITTY LEAGUE
OFFICIAL
SCOREBOOK
CLARKSVILLE COLTS
1949   10c

CLARKSVILLE BASEBALL CLUB

HORACE "HOD" LISENBEE. Owner and manager of the Colts, Lisenbee also pitched 75 innings with five complete games at the age of 50 in 1949. The Clarksville native spent six major-league seasons with the Washington Senators, Boston Red Sox, Philadelphia Athletics, and Cincinnati Reds from 1927 to 1945. He was a reliever and spot starter for the Reds in his final major-league season at age 46. (Walt Mestan.)

A muddy day at Fairfield Park

BURNING THE INFIELD. These photographs show a common method Kitty League groundskeepers used to make a muddy infield and pitching mound playable. They would spray gallons of gasoline on the dirt and set it on fire! Initially it created a crusty surface, but during the course of a game it would become muddy once again. (Dr. Curtis L. Englebright.)

P.S. It was still MUDDY!!

1950 MAYFIELD CLOTHIERS. Mayfield won the pennant for the first time since 1939 and advanced to the playoff finals. Danny Kravitz had 17 home runs and 102 RBIs and would later play five major-league seasons, mostly with the Pittsburgh Pirates, from 1956 to 1960. Neil Huff batted .302 with 22 stolen bases and 96 runs scored. Pitcher Dick McIntyre made the Kitty League All-Star Team with 14 victories.

1950 FULTON RAILROADERS. The second-place Railroaders made it into the playoff finals against Mayfield before bad weather canceled the series. Pictured are, from left to right, (first row) manager Ivan Kuester, Carroll "Pete" Peterson, Perry "Tex" Brown, Ralph "Chicken" Brawner, John Bohna, Charles Tate, and Harley Grossman; (second row) Paul Walther, Milton McEneny, Cecil Hubbard, Leonard Addison, James Jarrett, Leonard Korressel, and Frank Wiecek; (third row) Ralph Beckering, Ned Waldrop, and Jack Leonard; Larry Kuester is the batboy.

1950 OWENSBORO OILERS. Managed by future Hall of Famer Travis Jackson, the fourth-place Oilers lost to Mayfield in the first round of the playoffs. Joe Andrews won the batting title (.373). Pictured are, from left to right, (first row) Don McMahon, Gene Browning, an unidentified batboy, Neil Howard, and Joe Andrews; (second row) Keith Mason, Bud Jordan, Dan Mazurek, George Kornack, Gene Bauer, Lloyd Freund, Tyler Robinson, Bob Giusti, Terry Cramer, Earl Hamann, and manager Travis Jackson; (Earl Hamann.)

DON MCMAHON. A right-handed pitcher from Brooklyn, New York, McMahon led the Kitty League with a 20-9 record, 2.72 ERA, and 143 strikeouts with Owensboro in 1950 and was named to the Kitty League All-Star team. He went on to pitch in 18 major-league seasons, mostly with the Milwaukee Braves and San Francisco Giants, from 1957 to 1974. (Ronnie Peach.)

1950 JACKSON GENERALS. The relocated Clarksville franchise finished in third place and lost to Fulton in the first round of the playoffs. Pictured are, from left to right, (first row) Bearl Brooks, Walt Mestan, Len Addison, Hayden Ray, batboy Billy Reed, Don Stevens, Dick Janasky, Dominic Italiano, and Leo Martindale; (second row) Doyle Pruett, Bob Evans, Mike Conovan, Roy Walkup, Ed Krieger, Glen "Gabby" Stewart, Lee Valadez, Maurice Partain, and David Ross. (Walt Mestan.)

MAURICE PARTAIN. The Nashville, Tennessee, native came within one stolen base of tying the league record for stolen bases on the last day of the 1950 season but finished with 83. He played five seasons in the Kitty League with Clarksville and Jackson, hitting .298 with 219 stolen bases in 431 games. (Walt Mestan.)

TURNER FIELD. Above is a photograph of Turner Field in Union City, Tennessee, taken from atop the grandstand in 1952. It was definitely a pitcher's ballpark with a spacious outfield that was 437 feet in left-center and 424 feet in right-center from home plate. It featured a stone wall from right-center over to the right-field corner and rock-built dugouts deep enough in the ground that players on the bench were at eye-level with the playing field. The photograph below shows the stone outfield wall, the only part of Turner Field still standing today.

Back Row
George Busch, John Bohna, Jerry Dale, Vernon Curtis, Al. Brown, Don Menner, Walt Bryja
Front Row
Ned Waldrop, Jake Propst, Sam Lamitina, Andy Sventko, Billy Jo Forrest,
Mgr.
Milt McEneny, Reed Maier

1951 FULTON RAILROADERS. Led by first-year manager Sam Lamitina, the Railroaders won their first pennant since the abbreviated 1942 season and took four straight games from Owensboro in the playoff finals. Pictured are, from left to right, (first row) Ned Waldrop, Jake Propst, manager Sam Lamitina, Andy Sventko, Billy Joe Forrest, Milt McEneny, and Reed Maier; (second row) George Busch, John Bohna, Jerry Dale, Vernon "Turkey" Curtis, Alvin Brown, Don Menner, and Walt Bryja. Three-quarters of the all-star infield was made up of Railroaders: first baseman Ned Waldrop (.325, 12 home runs, 97 RBIs), second baseman Milt McEneny (.284, 93 runs), and shortstop and Fulton native Billy Joe Forrest (.255, 79 RBIs, 76 runs). Right-hander Walt Bryja led the league with 24 victories.

BIG NED. Ned Waldrop was the greatest hitter in Kitty League history. In seven seasons, he batted .337 with 110 home runs and 727 RBIs in 719 games. His best individual season was in 1954 when he hit .380, led the league with 22 home runs, and set a new single-season record of 159 RBIs. Waldrop was inducted into the Kitty League Hall of Fame in 2005. (Lydia Waldrop and family.)

STORMY SAM. One of the most successful managers in league history, Sam Lamitina won three consecutive pennants in 1951, 1952, and 1953. His managerial record with Fulton was 242-159 in four seasons. His hard-nosed brand of baseball and fiery temperament often clashed with opposing players and umpires. Lamitina was inducted into the Kitty League Hall of Fame in 2005. (Lydia Waldrop and family.)

WAYNE BLACKBURN. Blackburn started his professional career with the Paducah Indians in 1936 and returned to the league as player-manager of the Owensboro Oilers in 1951. The 37-year-old won the batting title with a .364 average, scoring 116 runs and stealing 26 bases. Blackburn later managed and scouted in the Detroit Tigers organization. (Ronnie Peach.)

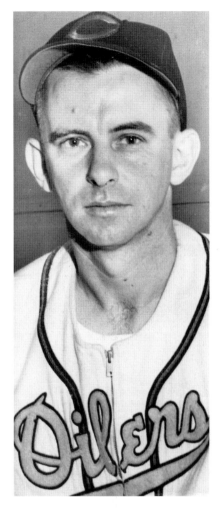

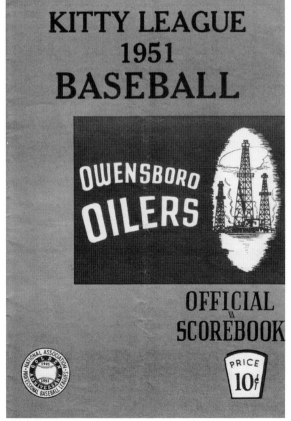

1951 OWENSBORO OILERS SCORECARD. The Oilers finished in second place but lost to Fulton in the final series of the playoffs. Marvin Donaldson batted .326 with 13 home runs and 92 RBIs. John Itace hit .318, and J.T. Jaynes drove in 81 runs. Robert Fiocchi had a 22-8 record with a 3.28 ERA, and Bobby Foster finished at 16-10.

J. POLK BROOKS AND EWING HAYDEN.
As president of the Paducah Baseball
Association, James Polk Brooks (left) was
the driving force behind the construction
of a new concrete and steel stadium that
fans named in his honor. After two seasons
in the Mississippi-Ohio Valley League, the
Chiefs returned to the Kitty League in
1951. Here, Brooks and business manager
Ewing Hayden model the team's home
and road uniforms. (Carol Brooks.)

1951 PADUCAH CHIEFS INFIELDERS. The Chiefs finished in fourth place but lost to Fulton
in the first round of the playoffs. Player-manager Bob Stanton (left) batted .248 in 48 games.
Second baseman Sam Goody hit .256 with 47 RBIs. Third baseman Russell Davis hit .298 with
34 doubles, 104 runs scored, and 16 stolen bases. First baseman Fred Koenig batted .261 in 29
games. (Karen Stanton Glisson.)

OPENING DAY

Sponsored by the Local
LIONS CLUB

GENERAL ADMISSION
Hoppers vs. Paducah

MONDAY NIGHT, MAY 7 1951
7:30 P. M.

*　　*　　*　　GOOD FOR ANY GAME OF SEASO

1951 OPENING-DAY TICKET. The Hopkinsville Lions Club sold 718 of these general admission tickets for the Hoppers' May 7 home opener against the Paducah Chiefs. Despite chilly weather, around 1,000 fans attended the game at Kentucky Park and saw the home team defeat Paducah 5-1. (William Turner collection.)

SOUVENIR PROGRAM

ALL – STAR GAME

JULY 24, 1951

FAIRFIELD PARK FULTON, KY.

1951 ALL-STAR GAME SCORECARD. Because the Fulton Railroaders were in first place after the Fourth of July, the small Kentucky town earned the privilege of hosting the Kitty League All-Star Game on July 24. Hal Seawright of the Jackson Generals went five for five with a home run, two doubles, and four RBIs in the Kitty League All-Stars' 6-2 victory over the Railroaders. Former baseball commissioner Happy Chandler was honored before the game.

KITTY  LEAGUE

MEMBER NATIONAL ASSOCIATION OF PROFESSIONAL BASEBALL CLUBS
ORGANIZED 1903

GEORGE M. TRAUTMAN, PRESIDENT NATIONAL ASS'N.   W. B. CARPENTER, CHIEF UMPIRE BUREAU

SHELBY PEACE, PRES.   ALLEN CLOAR, VICE-PRES.   VERA FUQUA, SEC'Y.   GLADSTONE MAJOR, TREAS.

HOPKINSVILLE, KY.

DIRECTORS—

WALTER CHAMNESS, PRES.
EGBERT A. SMITH, VICE-PRES.
PEYTON BERBLING, SECY.
C. W. BERBLING, TREAS.
CAIRO, ILL.

K. P. DALTON, PRES.
F. A. HOMRA, VICE-PRES.
W. W. EVANS, SEC'Y-TREAS.
H. H. BUGG, BUS. MGR.
FULTON, KY.

BILLY GOFF, PRES.
PEGGY GOFF, TREAS.
HOPKINSVILLE, KY.

SIMPSON RUSSELL, PRES.
SAM WAHL, VICE-PRES.
AARON ROBINSON, TREAS.
RUSSELL RICE, EXE. SEC.
JACKSON, TENN.

GEORGE R. MILLS, PRES.
WM. A. NISBET, VICE-PRES.
A. R. CUMMINGS, SECY.
MADISONVILLE, KY.

J. D. MYERS, PRES.
JACK ANDERSON, VICE-PRES.
DORIS STIMSON, SECY.
ACREE AUSTIN, BUS. MGR.
MAYFIELD, KY.

HARRY JENKINS, PRES.
WM. ARMSTRONG, VICE-PRES.
JOHN QUINN, TREAS.
RICHARD SILLS, BUS. MGR.
OWENSBORO, KY.

ANDY ANDERSON, PRES.
GUY WELDON, VICE-PRES.
TOM ELAM, SEC'Y-TREAS.
J. T. WITHERSPOON, BUS. MGR.
UNION CITY, TENN.

J. P. FRIEND STATISTICIAN
BLYTHEVILLE, ARK.

WOMAN'S PROMOTIONAL
DIVISION—

MISS MAMIE GATES,
MRS. MILDRED HANCOCK,
MRS. GEORGE FUNK,
HOPKINSVILLE, KY.

UMPIRES CHIEF ADVISER
HARRY 'STEAMBOAT' JOHNSON

July 12, 1951

Mr. Curtis Englebright
Union City Baseball Club
Union City, Tennessee

Dear Curtis:

You have been chosen third baseman on the
All-Star Team in the game between the Kitty
League All Stars and the Fulton Railroaders
on Tuesday, July 24, 7:45 p. m. at Fulton.

I want to congratulate you for having been
chosen and I trust that I shall see you at
the game.

Sincerely,

Shelby Peace

SHELBY PEACE
President

SP:vbf

1951 ALL-STAR GAME INVITATION. This is the invitation from league president Shelby Peace to third baseman Curt Englebright of the Union City Greyhounds informing him of his election to the Kitty League All-Star Team. (Curtis L. Englebright.)

1952 FULTON LOOKOUTS. The Lookouts won their second straight pennant in convincing fashion with an 82-37 record and .689 winning percentage, the best ever for a Kitty League team. Howard Weeks (back row, third from left) won the batting title with a .370 average and drove in 98 runs. Ned Waldrop (back row, far left) hit .357 with 103 RBIs. Pitcher Alvin Brown (back row, second from right) won 25 games, and Don Menner (back row, second from left) went 16-1. (Lydia Waldrop and family.)

1952 FULTON LOOKOUTS SCORECARD. Fulton changed its nickname from the Railroaders to the Lookouts in 1952 and began wearing uniforms handed down from the Chattanooga Lookouts, the Washington Senators' Double-A affiliate. Among the advertisers in the scorecard were H.H. Bugg Grocery (owned by club's business manager) and Simons Paint and Wallpaper Store, owned by former Fulton player and major-leaguer Mel Simons. (Michael Risley.)

HOWARD WEEKS. The left-handed hitting outfielder won back-to-back batting titles in 1952 (.370) and 1953 (.373) in two championship seasons for the Lookouts. A native of Pine Bluff, Arkansas, Weeks hit .336 with 48 home runs and 320 RBIs in 371 games. (Martha Weeks.)

1952 OPENING-DAY TICKET. This ticket allowed general admission seating to see the Hopkinsville Hoppers beat the Paducah Chiefs 3-1 at Kentucky Park on May 4. Members of the Hopper Service Club, a ladies' booster organization, presented players with a large cake during pregame ceremonies. (William Turner collection.)

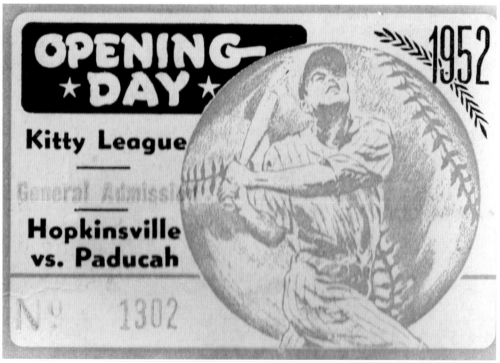

1952 MADISONVILLE MINERS. The third-place Miners beat Paducah three games to one and swept Union City in three to win the playoffs. Pictured are, from left to right, (first row) Everett Robinson, Tom Flanigan, Carmen Troisi, Hal McGahey, Leonard Johnston, and Dick Heighs; (second row) Bill Witmer, Jim Rentschler, Ted Lesko, Mel Rainey, and Don Hefelfinger; (third row) Don Drake, Tom Pritchard, Ed Rellegert, Robert Walz, and Neil Roberts; Roy Day is the batboy. (Bill Witmer.)

MADISONVILLE MINERS CLUBHOUSE. There were few amenities in a typical Kitty League clubhouse. It was often close, damp quarters for 15 or more players, and showers were considered a luxury. This is a rare photograph from 1952 of the home clubhouse beneath the first-base stands at Madisonville's Municipal Stadium. (Steve Brown.)

On Deck. This is a rare photograph of a Kitty League game in progress in 1952. The on-deck hitter for the Madisonville Miners is Leonard Johnston, who batted .353 in 61 games. (Steve Brown.)

Carmen Troisi. The Madisonville Miners shortstop poses beside the home dugout at Municipal Stadium in Madisonville, Kentucky. Troisi batted .285 in 64 games with the Miners in 1952. The grandstand behind him is still standing. (Steve Brown.)

1952 OWENSBORO OILERS. The Oilers finished the season in fifth place, 27.5 games behind Fulton. Catcher Jack Hall batted .321 with a league-best 21 home runs and 136 RBIs, and all-star third baseman Howard Harkins batted .244 with 16 stolen bases. Minor-league home-run hitter D.C. "Pud" Miller began the season as manager but hit only seven homers in 48 games. (Ronnie Peach.)

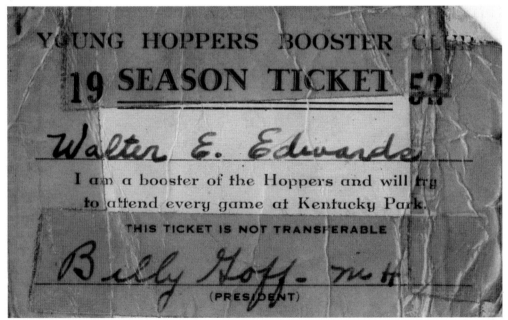

1952 YOUNG HOPPERS SEASON TICKET. Shown here is a Young Hoppers Booster Club membership card belonging to a fan named Walter E. Edwards. Signed by team president Billy Goff, it was used to encourage attendance by younger fans—and no doubt encourage their parents to come to Kentucky Park as well. (William Turner collection.)

FAN FAVORITES. Hopkinsville Hoppers third baseman Tony Sarno (left) and outfielder Art Sabulsky pose with local fans Gary Tuttle (reading the comic book) and Jimmy Sivils (between Sarno's knees) beside the batting cage at Kentucky Park in 1952. A New Jersey native, Sarno batted .259 with 29 RBIs. Sabulsky was from Pittsburgh, Pennsylvania, and hit .256 with 55 RBIs.

VOICE OF THE HOPPERS. Leo Wilson began his broadcasting career as an engineer for WHOP, Hopkinsville's first radio station, in 1940. Over the next 20 years, he was well known as the choice for local sporting events, including play-by-play accounts of the Hopkinsville Hoppers. Leo was the voice of the Hoppers from 1946 to 1954. He and his wife, Mary, still live in Hopkinsville, Kentucky.

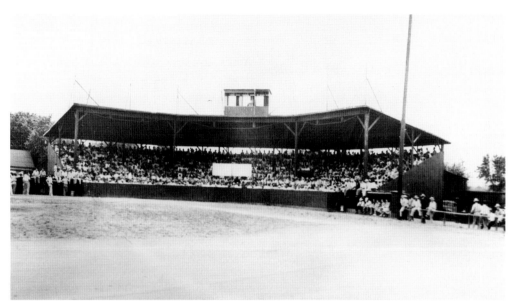

KENTUCKY PARK. Here is a view of the grandstand from left field at Kentucky Park in Hopkinsville, Kentucky. Built partially with lumber from the pre–World War II Mercer Park grandstand, it was constructed by team owner Billy Goff before the 1946 season. (William Turner collection.)

GAME AT KENTUCKY PARK. In this photograph, the visiting Fulton Railroaders are batting against the Hoppers. The on-deck hitter with no. 16 on his jersey is Railroaders' first baseman Ned Waldrop. (Lydia Waldrop and family.)

THE KITTY LEAGUE

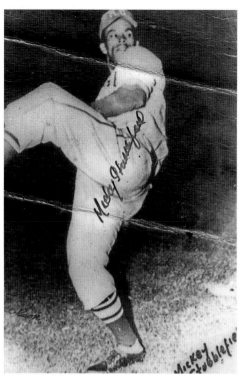

MICKEY STUBBLEFIELD. A Mayfield native, Stubblefield became the first African American player in Kitty League history when he pitched for the hometown Clothiers against the Paducah Chiefs on June 26, 1952, and won 5-4. Other towns, with the exception of Paducah and Jackson, would not allow him to pitch in their ballparks. Pitching all but one game in his hometown, Stubblefield finished the season with a 7-6 record and 3.70 ERA.

1952 MAYFIELD CLOTHIERS. With the addition of Mickey Stubblefield, former major-league pitcher Frank "Red" Barrett managed the first integrated team in the Kitty League. The Pittsburgh Pirates' farm club finished in last place with a 47-70 record. Nicholas Ferrante led the team with 10 home runs, 10 triples, and 71 RBIs. Kenneth Meyer batted .311, and Frank Wilburn had a 10-11 record. (Mickey Stubblefield.)

1952 PADUCAH CHIEFS SCORECARD. The Chiefs produced a slick 18-page scorecard with illustrations of an Indian chief and St. Louis Cardinals logo to show their major-league affiliate. After paying 10¢ for the scorecard, fans at Brooks Stadium could purchase a red hot dog for 20¢ and a bag of peanuts or popcorn for 10¢. A soft drink sold for 10¢ and cold beer for 25¢.

1952 UNION CITY GREYHOUNDS. The Greyhounds finished in fourth place. They beat the Lookouts in the first round of the playoffs but lost three straight to Madisonville in the finals. Pictured are, from left to right, (first row) Dewey Martling and Walt Dziedzic; (second row) Frank Radler, Lloyd Woodling, Ed Knapp, Dick Coffman, Art Cook, and Sherwood "Lefty" Lessig; (third row) Chico Cortez, John Bohna, Bob Carlson, J.T. Jaynes, Jay Stasko, John Rothenhausler, and Bob Oefinger. (Lynn Rothenhausler.)

50TH-ANNIVERSARY PATCH. The Kitty League celebrated its golden anniversary throughout the 1953 season (although it had actually played only 28 seasons at that point). As part of the celebration, players and managers wore this commemorative patch on their sleeves designed by second baseman Jay Stasko of the Union City Dodgers.

GOLDEN ANNIVERSARY ADVERTISEMENT. This is a page from the 1953 Madisonville Miners program with local advertisements and recognition of the Kitty League's 50th anniversary.

HOPKINSVILLE BASEBALL CLUB, Inc.

MEMBER KITTY LEAGUE

Affiliated with Philadelphia Athletics

RUSS MELVIN,
President—General Manager

HOPKINSVILLE, KY.

W. N. McKINNEY,
V. President—Secretary-Treasurer

October 31, 1953

Mr. Billy Goff
% H.B. Shelton Motors
Hopkinsville, Ky.

Dear Billy:

This is to inform you, as per our lease, that the Hopkinsville
Baseball Club, Inc., will want to renew its lease on Kentucky
Park for the 1954 season.

Incidentally, it looks rough right now for the Kitty League
next year. Three clubs are in pretty shaky circumstances.

Sincerely yours,

Russ Melvin

Russ Melvin

TROUBLE AHEAD. This letter written by Hopkinsville Hoppers owner Russ Melvin on October 23, 1953, to former team owner Billy Goff mentions potential trouble for the Kitty League leading into the 1954 season. (William Turner collection.)

GOOD-LUCK HORSESHOE.
The Owensboro Oilers began their first season as an affiliate of the world champion New York Yankees in 1953. Manager Marvin Crater (right) accepts a good-luck horseshoe from a young fan on opening night at Miller Field, as Madisonville Miners skipper Everett Robinson looks on. The Oilers went on to beat the Miners 10-9. (Ronnie Peach.)

1953 FULTON LOOKOUTS. Fulton won its third consecutive pennant, setting a new Kitty League record. Though not as dominant as during the previous season, the Lookouts went 70-50 and made it to the final series of the playoffs. Pitcher Ronald "Mickey" Foster won 21 games, the third consecutive season that a Fulton hurler led the league in victories. Howard Weeks (back row, third from left) won his second straight batting title (.373). (Lydia Waldrop and family.)

1953 MADISONVILLE MINERS SCORECARD.
The Miners finished in second place but lost
to the Paducah Chiefs in the initial round of
the playoffs. Manager Everett Robinson batted
.296 with 97 RBIs. All-star Rodriguez Arias won
16 games with a league-leading 247 strikeouts.
Joe Hicks batted .389 with 16 homers in 67
games but did not qualify for the batting title.
He played five seasons in the major leagues.

POSTGAME CELEBRATION. Paducah Chiefs catcher Bill Weddle (left) and relief pitcher Gene
Puckett celebrate a victory during the 1953 season. Weddle hit .284 in 62 games, and Puckett
had an 11-9 record with 152 strikeouts. The third-place Chiefs (67-53) swept the league champion
Fulton Lookouts in three straight games to win the postseason championship. (Gene Puckett.)

1953 HOPKINSVILLE HOPPERS. Despite a 59-60 record, the Hoppers finished in third place and made it into the playoffs. Leo Bacon won 13 games. Pictured are, from left to right, (first row) manager Norm Wilson, Bill Kasper, Bob Brown, Harold Crotts, Sam Germano, Steve Durst, Leo Bacon, Marvin Lowe, Tommy Williamson, and Jim Wilson; (second row) Pete Harbold, John Dugan, Howard "Boots" Warrell, Stan Somers, Tommy Jasonis, and Skip Fiscel. (William Turner collection.)

ALL-STAR SLUGGERS. Hopkinsville Hoppers Howard "Boots" Warrell (left) and Harold "Hal" Crotts were both named to the Kitty League All-Star Team in 1953. Warrell batted .334, tied for the league home-run title with 26, scored a league-best 113 runs, and drove in 129 runs. Crotts hit .336 with 19 homers and 116 RBIs and had a 26-game hitting streak during the season. (Howard Warrell.)

1953 JACKSON GENERALS. The Cincinnati Reds farm club, managed by George "Mickey" O'Neil, finished in sixth place. Ray D'Agrosa won 14 games. The men pictured are, from left to right, (first row) Ritchie Roth, Howard Whitson, Charles "Chick" Re, Eddie Miller, manager O'Neil, Gene Bennett, Carroll Drostie, Dick Wehman, and Dominic Italiano; (second row) Earl Gearhardt, Vince Monaco, Bill Newkirk, Ray D'Agrosa, George McLeod, Ivan Mills, Jerry Elder, and John Scercy. (Jim Bailey.)

1953 OWENSBORO OILERS. Before the season began, it appeared the Oilers were finished after club directors turned the franchise over to the league. Local fans and city leaders created a nonprofit organization to operate the team and had the highest attendance in the eight-club circuit at 64,375 despite a last-place finish. Manager Marvin Crater (second row, far right) led the Oilers with a .357 average, 31 doubles, and 70 RBIs. (Ronnie Peach.)

1954 Union City Dodgers. The Brooklyn farm club won the pennant, and Al Shinn won the batting title with a .391 average. Pictured are, from left to right, (first row) Bill Liberto, Sal DeMatteis, Bob Kozcawra, Buckie Russell, Al Costa, Gene "Shorty" Dearman, and Jim Major; (second row) Bill Saar, Al Shinn, Rene Masip, Ed Allen, Bob Vertich, Joe Fernandez, Tom Sheridan, Lowell Mendenhall, Earl Naylor, and Chuck Templeton; Buster Thomas is the batboy. (Al Shinn.)

Three Decades of Batting Champions. This special photograph was taken at the Kitty League Centennial Reunion in Paducah, Kentucky, in August 2003. Each of the gentleman pictured won the league batting title: David Bartosch (left) batted .337 for the Union City Greyhounds in 1937, Lester Severin (center) batted .381 for the Cairo Egyptians in 1948, and Al Shinn batted .391 for the Union City Dodgers in 1954. (Photograph by Trace Kirkwood.)

1954 MADISONVILLE MINERS. The Miners captured the second-half title but lost the championship playoff to Union City four games to two. All-star Bill Pass led the league with 162 hits and batted .351 with 101 runs scored. Fellow all-star Frank Layana hit .357 with 10 home runs and almost had a no-hitter against Hopkinsville on July 30, 1954, in a pitching stint. Bill Johnson went 15-6 with 148 strikeouts. (Steve Brown.)

HOPKINSVILLE HOPPERS STOCK CERTIFICATE. In February 1954, local fans formed the Hopkinsville Community Baseball Club and took over the franchise from out-of-town owner W.N. McKinney to ensure baseball would be played at Kentucky Park. Local physician Dr. J.W.F. Williams did his part during the fundraising drive and purchased a single share of stock for $25. (William Turner collection.)

1954 OWENSBORO OILERS. The Oilers ended the first half in fifth place but finished second in the second half. Seventeen-year-old Tony Kubek (top row, third from left) led the team in batting (.344) on his way to careers as a major leaguer with the New York Yankees and a television broadcaster. Lee Thomas, another future big leaguer from 1961 to 1968, batted .304 in 68 games. All-stars Edward Dick and Dominick Maisano finished 7-0 and 10-5 respectively. (Ronnie Peach.)

EYE FOR BEAUTY. Paducah Indians second baseman Robert Nadeau (left) and a teammate pose beside an outfield advertising sign at Brooks Stadium in Paducah, Kentucky, in 1954. Nadeau played in 17 games with the Indians and batted .276. (Robert Nadeau.)

FULTON BALLPARK. The financial success of three consecutive pennants enabled the Fulton Baseball Association to tear down the wooden Fairfield Park grandstand and fence and build a new concrete block structure and outfield wall in its place. Renamed Fulton Ballpark, it opened in 1954 and hosted the Lookouts for the team's final two seasons in the Kitty League. (Lydia Waldrop and family.)

1955 PADUCAH CHIEFS. Paducah won the final league championship with a record of 64-39. Pictured are, from left to right, (first row) batboy Jerry Hoover, business manager Ewing Hayden, Gary Grosnickle, Hubert Phipps, Ray Wilson, club president J. Polk Brooks, and batboy Charles Hipkiss; (second row) Jack Ramsey, Dick Gentry, Bill Silverthorne, Tom Baker, Don Catchot, and Ron Leandri; (third row) Thad Jennings, Jake DeSousa, Jim McKnight, Darold Satchell, Mike O'Conner, and Al Smith. (Jerry Hoover.)

The **Kitty League** 18

OF PROFESSIONAL BASEBALL CLUBS

1955

EXTENDS THE COURTESY OF ALL ITS GROUNDS

To HELEN KING & PARTY

PADUCAH, KY.
MADISONVILLE, KY.
MAYFIELD, KY.
FULTON, KY.
OWENSBORO, KY.
UNION CITY, TENN.

Shelby Peace

PRESIDENT

Not Transferable

1955 SEASON PASS. The 1955 season would be the last for the Kitty League. Attendance had dropped steadily since 1950, and the league went into the season with only six clubs before going to an uneven five-team arrangement after Madisonville folded on July 7. With five days left in the season, Mayfield, Owensboro, and Union City declined to participate in the postseason Shaughnessy playoffs and forfeited the playoff title to first-place Paducah.

1955 MAYFIELD CLOTHIERS SCORECARD. The New York Giants farm club finished in second place. Ed Herstek led the league at .359, and Paul Bentley belted 14 home runs. Joe Shipley won 13 games and pitched four seasons in the major leagues. Manager Dave Garcia later skippered the California Angels and Cleveland Indians from 1977 to 1982 and was a major-league coach for the Milwaukee Brewers and Colorado Rockies.

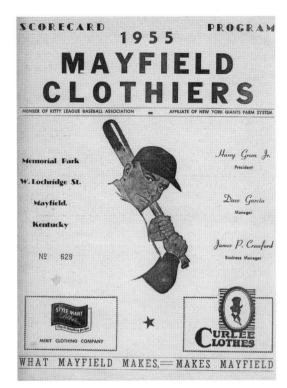

LAST NO-HITTER. On June 17, 1955, Madisonville Miners left-hander Jack Kralick pitched the last no-hitter in Kitty League history, a 1-0 victory over the Union City Dodgers. He tossed a seven-inning gem a year later for Duluth-Superior in the Northern League. Kralick pitched for the Washington Senators, Minnesota Twins, and Cleveland Indians from 1959 to 1967. With the Twins, he had a no-hit game against the Kansas City Athletics on August 26, 1962.

MILLER FIELD. This photograph harkens back to its glory days when it was custom before the start of every game for the announcer to thank Roy's Place across the street for turning off its bright neon sign. On September 19, 1955, Miller Field was demolished to make way for a shopping center. One supporter candidly said, "It's too valuable a piece of land for a baseball park." (Ronnie Peach.)

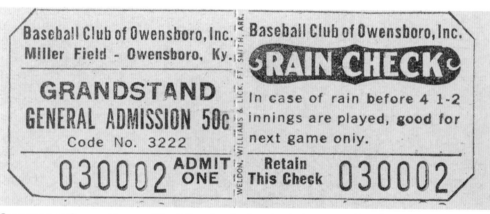

OWENSBORO OILERS TICKET. The Oilers finished in third place in 1955. All-star Joe Cintron was the leading batter with a .325 average and 60 RBIs. Manager Walter Lane contributed 66 RBIs in 85 games before he was replaced in August by former major leaguer Ken Silvestri. Pitcher Arnold Briggs led the team with a 15-5 record, and David Palmer won all-star honors with a 6-11 record and 3.27 ERA. (Ronnie Peach.)

SHELBY PEACE. The Hopkinsville native first became associated with the Kitty League as a 17-year-old fan operating the manual scoreboard and acting as batboy for his hometown team in 1903. As an adult, he helped league president Dr. Frank Bassett resurrect the circuit from periods of dormancy and was scorekeeper for the Hopkinsville clubs. During the 1935–1942 revival, Peace became league secretary and vice president before being elected to the presidency in 1941. He brought the circuit back in 1946 and guided it during an eight-year period of stability and prosperity. He lamented the intrusion of major-league radio broadcasts into minor-league territory and attributed its "highly dramatic and plumb silly" descriptions of the game to the league's eventual demise in 1955. Fans knew with Peace's death in 1958 that the Kitty League itself was truly gone. (Marshall Peace.)

DISCOVER THOUSANDS OF LOCAL HISTORY BOOKS
FEATURING MILLIONS OF VINTAGE IMAGES

Arcadia Publishing, the leading local history publisher in the United States, is committed to making history accessible and meaningful through publishing books that celebrate and preserve the heritage of America's people and places.

Find more books like this at
www.arcadiapublishing.com

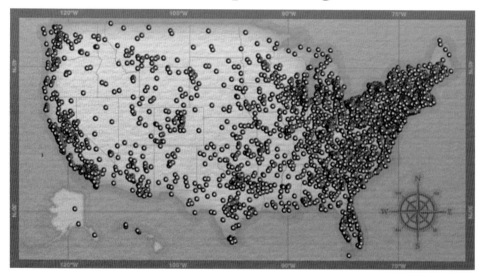

Search for your hometown history, your old stomping grounds, and even your favorite sports team.